Thanks for the year... friendship. 5/1/69

JUVENILE JUSTICE GUIDE

Ed Thibault

EDWARD A. THIBAULT, Ph.D.
AND JOHN J. MACERI, M.S.W.

Edward A. Thibault
John J. Maceri

i

Library of Congress Cataloging-in-Publication Data

Thibault, Edward A., 1939-
    Juvenile justice guide / Edward A. Thibault and John J. Maceri.
        p. cm.
    Includes bibliographical references.
    ISBN 978-1-932777-76-5
        1. Juvenile justice, Administration of--United States. 2. Juvenile courts--United States. 3. Juvenile delinquency--United States. I. Maceri, John J. II. Title.
    KF9780.T46 2009
    345.73'08--dc22

                                                        2009002568

Cover and interior design by Sans Serif Inc., Saline, Michigan

Dedication

This is dedicated to Anthony J. Maceri for all the years he was a loyal brother and great friend. The authors are positive he would have truly enjoyed seeing our book in print.

Contents

Contents

Contents

Contents

Contents

Contents

The Authors

John J Maceri, M.S.W. has been Regional Administrator, providing training and management consultation for 33 probation agencies through the New York State Probation and Correctional Alternatives Division. He brought in new and innovative programs to these 33 agencies. His career in probation spans 40 years including many years of adult and juvenile cases, work and field experiences. He taught Community Corrections and the Senior Seminar in the Public Justice Department at SUNY, Oswego, for over 25 years. He is widely respected in the field of probation for his humanity and knowledge of community corrections, the law and management.

Edward A. Thibault, Ph.D., a professor and scholar in Criminal Justice, created the Public Justice degree at SUNY, Oswego, and is a co-founder and former president of the Criminal Justice Educators Association of New York State and the Northeastern Association of Criminal Justice Sciences, a college faculty association covering New England through Washington, D.C., and the nearest Canadian Provinces. Professor Thibault taught Juvenile Delinquency for over thirty years at SUNY, Oswego, and was chair of the Sociology Department. He published 26 articles including newsletters; delivered 32 scholarly papers, organized ten regional criminal justice conferences including publishing a major article on juvenile justice in *Crime and Delinquency.* His *Proactive Police Management* textbook has been in print since 1985, is in its seventh edition, and is used at Harvard and two- and four-year colleges all over America. The text is one of four textbooks that are required reading for police promotional civil service tests in the state of Massachusetts. Dr. Thibault is a proven leader in criminal justice higher education.

Acknowledgments

The authors thank the professionals who read and helped edit the original manuscript. It took over a year to rewrite, add materials and reorganize. It has come out clearer, more readable and a fine book full of useful information. We owe much of these positive changes to our four reviewers. They are:

Richard A. Smith, lawyer and professional government consultant who had a critical eye for helping us correct errors in both content and writing. We appreciate the hours he spent with the manuscript.

Marilyn Miller (Marilyn Westlake), a lawyer/mediator in New York State Family Court who had an eagle eye for problems in the manuscript, helping us wrestle with the legal and ethical content. She especially contributed to smoothing out the writing. We also appreciate the hours she spent with the manuscript.

Richard Nells, a major administrator for New York State Youth and Family Services, former Probation Director and County Executive gave us recommendations and changes for the manuscript from his unique perspective.

John Sutton, Director of Chemung County Probation in New York State and his staff went over the manuscript recommending changes and giving us a perspective from the viewpoint of local probation.

Marianne Thibault is thanked for the emotional support she gave her husband/writer Edward Thibault, while he and John Maceri toiled over the manuscript for three years.

Introduction:
How To Use This Guide

The Juvenile Justice Guide is a practical handbook for people and professionals involved in the juvenile justice system and is a fine supplement for Juvenile Delinquency and Juvenile Justice courses. Parents, guardians and troubled youths who are the most affected by the Juvenile Justice system have a special need for timely and accurate information. The *Guide* was carefully written and edited in order to provide easily understood information about the Juvenile Justice system. To obtain this goal, the Guide has a minimum of footnotes and scholarly references.

Probation officers, juvenile parole officers, police officers, lawyers, social workers, youth workers and other professionals will find this *Guide* to be especially helpful. Some law schools do not provide a course in juvenile justice, so lawyers are in special need of good information and guidance in juvenile justice. When this *Guide* is used for training, everyone needs to own a personal copy for future reference.

Law courses, law schools, criminal justice courses, criminology, juvenile justice and juvenile delinquency courses will use the *Juvenile Justice Guide* as a brief and clear description of juvenile justice. The *Guide* is a fine supplementary text. Parents, adolescents and professionals with juvenile clients and children in the system will find the *Juvenile Justice Guide* especially helpful. Students, social workers and criminal justice professionals should save the *Juvenile Justice Guide* as a basic reference for their careers.

Juvenile courts have many responsibilities. This book is focusing on persons in need of supervision (PINS), juvenile delinquents (JD's) and the process of going through the juvenile justice system. The book will look at child abuse and neglect as it effects the juveniles being taken out of their homes and becoming delinquent. The juvenile court also deals with adoptions, custody, and appointment of guardians and can take away parental rights for cause.

The *Guide* does not cover divorce, child support, or custody. The focus is the troubled juvenile who has become officially involved with the juvenile justice system. Juvenile court is a court where the district attorney normally prosecutes adolescents and children. These juveniles may commit crimes like armed robbery but they are never convicted of a crime as juveniles. They are adjudicated as juvenile delinquents or persons in need of supervision. Depending on the state, juveniles are adjudicated for committing non-criminal status acts under various headings in different states which is explained in chapter one. These "persons in need of supervision" juveniles may have skipped school or run away from home, for example. Although there are other labels for juveniles who commit status acts, the *Juvenile Justice Guide* will use PINS, persons in need of supervision, for convenience.

Knowing the differences between the adult criminal justice system and the juvenile justice system is essential since most people and professionals are only familiar with the adult criminal justice system. Practical advice is needed for the whole family. Members of the family also need to understand how relationships within the family affects troubled juveniles. Parents and guardians have clear responsibilities in the court process and in helping the troubled juvenile make a positive change in behavior. The juvenile justice process is described in detail because of the lifelong consequences for both parents and juveniles.

United States Supreme Court cases have a profound effect on the process and the fairness of the juvenile justice system. Juveniles have fewer constitutional rights than adults. What rights juveniles have are determined by these court cases. Sentences, placements, counseling approaches and programs are described so that we all know what is happening to our adolescents, children and grandchildren. Everyone involved needs to have an idea of what works and what doesn't work.

There is a need to know more about the juvenile justice system by parents, the public and the juveniles in the system. The Juvenile Justice System has been hidden from the public for too many years. There are government and journalistic reports, juvenile delinquency and juvenile justice college courses; otherwise the public is generally excluded from the juvenile justice system. Most juvenile judges never open their courts to the public and the media.

The *Juvenile Justice Guide* is scholarly and accurate. The authors have over seventy years of experience and scholarship in the field between them. This is first and foremost a ***practical*** guide to the juvenile justice system in the United States with practical consequences for all of us. Our children and grandchildren are the future of our country and we need to encourage them to adopt the values of a positive life style.

Overview of the Chapters

Each chapter is written so the reader can have immediate access to essential information and apply this information to individual juveniles and juvenile cases. The *Guide* is to be used by parents and their sons or daughters who become involved in the juvenile justice system. Lawyers are assigned juvenile cases when they have little knowledge of how the juvenile justice system works. It is not fair to either the lawyers or their clients. Police officers may have had a juvenile justice or delinquency course in college, otherwise they usually do not have a clue of how the juvenile justice system works. Social workers, youth workers and probation officers have cases that become involved in the juvenile justice system and really need a clear introduction. A minimum of documentation is in the chapters in order to make this Guide easier to read. Documentation in the chapters refers to the bibliography and websites at the end of the book.

Chapter One covers the legal reasons for the juvenile coming to the attention of the juvenile justice system. Look at these reasons and the three case examples and see if your juvenile case fits. Next, look at the section on hiring a juvenile justice lawyer and hire an experienced lawyer. The court may appoint a lawyer to represent the juvenile in court. Ask the lawyer some of the questions listed in this chapter to see if they know anything about the juvenile justice system. Gather the information needed for a fair and complete social history. Examine the various assessments that will be used to apply the social history and what your juvenile did. You need to be especially vigilant about what is written in a predisposition report, which is a background history of the juvenile and his or her family. In any organization, most people will only know the juvenile through the paper work. Make sure this paperwork treats your juvenile's case in a fair and accurate manner.

Chapter Two treats the impact of the juvenile system on the juvenile's family. All juveniles grow up in a family and neighborhood. Even if the juvenile is taken out of the home, most juveniles will come back to that family and neighborhood. Everyone in the family as well as professionals who intervene in the family need to understand the 21st century changes in family relationships. The goal is to show how the family can support positive changes in the juvenile's future behavior. This is not easy to do. Read this chapter carefully and think about the needed relationship changes that are necessary.

Chapter Three shows what community based and institutional services are provided for juveniles and their family by various social services and probation. This includes both private agencies and government agencies. Everyone involved needs to have information on how these agencies operate and how to use their services. Diversion provides an approach for limiting the involvement of the juvenile in the juvenile legal system. This should be a goal of everyone involved. Sometimes, professionals in the system need to be made aware of this goal. There are directories of agencies in many communities. Look them up and gather information and ask questions. You may find additional services like psychological counseling and drug and alcohol professionals with competent reputations that can help your juvenile case. You also need to understand how judges and agency administrators send juveniles to specialized agencies and how transfers are made. One approach we embrace is having professionals sit down with a group of parents and explain the various placements to them.

Chapter Four describes how most juvenile and family courts operate according to what really is going on, as well as the official legal process. Most people have an understanding of adult criminal courts through civic classes, popular novels, the World Wide Web and television. **Juvenile court is different!** The chart on the comparison between juvenile legal proceedings and adult criminal legal proceedings explains the differences at a glance. You have to understand this to talk to lawyers, probation officers and professionals in the system. The juvenile, parents and even professionals and lawyers need to have this chapter carefully explained in order to understanding what is happening. Judgment of guilt or innocence and judgments about the juvenile's future will be made through this process. The language of juvenile court normally doesn't talk about guilt and innocence like adult court does. This chapter repeats some information from previous chapters. This is done to underscore the importance of the flow of cases and the decision-making process. Bring this *Guide* into court with you and ask questions if you need to understand what is going on. Every word in this chapter is important to your juvenile case.

Chapter Five helps us understand the historic meaning of juvenile justice in the United States and what constitutional rights the juvenile has been granted or denied by the U.S. Supreme Court. The conclusion of the 1967 In Re Gault case is the most important statement of juvenile rights. The last section summarizes the rights juveniles have and do not have today. Court appointed lawyers represent the juvenile and not the parents. This chapter has carefully outlined the rights of juveniles through U.S. Supreme Court cases that you and your lawyer can use in juvenile court.

Chapter Six describes the sentencing and placement choices juvenile judges can make once the juvenile has been judged guilty. In juvenile court language, guilty means that the juvenile has been adjudicated as **accepting the facts**. You may ask the courts through the juvenile's lawyer or through a probation officer for a specific placement you have researched. This is unusual but may help your juvenile case if you have good reasons. Otherwise read the placement section to understand what may happen to your juvenile case and why. The normal reasons for placing a juvenile anywhere is a need for certain services such as specific counseling needs and to protect the community through a secure enough placement. Try to find as much as possible about where your juvenile is placed and what kind of services would be available. If your juvenile is an alcoholic or drug addict and the placement has no drug or alcohol counseling, you would want a different placement. If you are a parent or guardian, you may ask for a placement close to your home so you can afford the time and money needed to visit your child.

Chapter Seven is a description of the different psychological approaches used by juvenile counselors. Group counseling is the most popular and least expensive counseling approach. Reviewing the various approaches, you might find one or more approach that is more apt to work with your juvenile. You can discuss this with the professionals involved in your juvenile case. It could be helpful in changing the juvenile's behavior for the positive. There are many other counseling approaches than those listed but these are historically the most used and taught in counseling programs. Different types of cognitive therapy and reality therapy, for example, have been popular. If a certain counseling approach doesn't work with juveniles, there is always another counselor and another approach. It takes some time to match the best counseling and the best counselor for a specific juvenile. We are all different and a troubled juvenile can be very difficult. All we can do is to try our best and hope for a positive change in behavior.

Chapter Eight is a summary of the major theories taught in college concerning delinquency and why young people become involved in antisocial behavior. Most of the reasons center around where adolescents grow up, family, friends and neighborhood. There is a great deal of fancy language in sociology theories but it doesn't change the reality of what the major influences are in our life as we grow up.

Differential Association talks about exposure to antisocial norms and says they become important in a young person's life in terms of how often the exposure, how intense the exposure and the earlier in a person's life the exposure, the more likely it is to have an important effect. It also says that we learn antisocial behavior from family and friends in the neighborhood and we do not get these antisocial notions through genetic inheritance. Ecological approaches stress bad neighborhoods, which may develop into antisocial, counter cultures where youths may become involved in criminal gangs. Control theory tells us that the more involved youths are in legitimate middle class behavior and values, the bigger the stake in the middle class community and the less likely these youths will become delinquent. To understand youths who get into trouble, it is important to understand what the young people are going through as they mature through adolescence. The newest theories combine the various delinquent theories and test them out in research projects as integrated theories.

Chapter Nine provides a wide variety of programs that have worked for juveniles over the last eighty years up to the present. Our selection process included examining the scientific empirical data showing a positive effect on juveniles. The positive change in behavior had to be statistically significant and not happen by chance, such as flipping a coin. We also liked a few programs that did not meet these scientific criteria and we said so. We also have pointed out three programs that did not work and that juveniles should not get involved with. Some of the programs in this chapter have helped parents with troubled juveniles. It is interesting reading. Look these programs over. You might find a program that will work for you or for your troubled juvenile. We have examined juvenile programs over time and have not chosen the most recent programs unless there are empirically verified data that shows that they work.

Chapter Ten peers into the future based on our scholarship and involvement with the juvenile justice system. The authors have thought long and hard to offer recommendations which will make the system fairer and work better for all of us. Besides understanding the rules and language of juvenile justice, we are all involved in supporting our youth emotionally and providing them with a brighter future.

If you have any suggestions for improvements or additions, e-mail the authors at drthibault@aol.com

1

Entering the Juvenile Justice System

Chapter Outline

Chapter 1

What Brings A Youth Into the Juvenile Justice System?

Breaking the law brings a juvenile in the juvenile justice system. Extralegal reasons for the behavior will be looked at, such as the family, neighborhood, individual personality, personal history, human services and the role of community standards.

Some reasons for the apprehension, arrest and referral to the juvenile justice system are similar as those for adults, for example, an illegal criminal act such as burglarizing a house. The language for the apprehension and arrest of juveniles differs from state to state. Some states may have similar terms or even the same terms for juvenile justice as other states. Juveniles who commit an act that would be a crime if they were an adult are considered juvenile delinquents.

Juveniles may also be transferred to the adult criminal courts for certain serious crimes, depending on the legal process and the laws in various states. The juvenile court may give up or waive its jurisdiction and transfer its authority over the youth to adult criminal court. Many states give original jurisdiction to adult court for certain serious crimes while other states let the district attorney decide where the case will be tried for these serious crimes. For example, New York State under the Juvenile Offender law, gives the adult criminal court original jurisdiction for murder at age 13 and for certain serious felonies for ages 14 and 15. The age at which a youth goes to an adult or juvenile court varies from state to state. When the adult court has jurisdiction over juveniles, the legal process will be different, depending on the specific laws in each state.

Most states consider 18 at the time the crime is committed to be the age when an act is considered an adult act rather than a juvenile act.

The Oldest age for juvenile court having original jurisdiction is:

- Age 15, three states, Connecticut, New York, and
  North Carolina;
- Age 16, ten states,
- Age 17, the rest of the states

As can be seen in this brief introduction, this is a complicated system that we are trying to simplify and outline so it is understandable. The *Juvenile Justice Guide* will use the terms juvenile and youth interchangeably without referring to the specific ages in each state.

Juveniles can be referred to the juvenile justice system for reasons other than adult criminal offenses. These offenses are commonly referred as status offenses. Some examples are failure to attend school under the age of sixteen, running away from home, under-age drinking alcoholic beverages, incorrigibility and being outside the home during curfew hours. Incorrigibility usually refers to juveniles having a pattern of not obeying parents or guardians and may include insulting and demeaning behavior in relation to their parents or guardians. A curfew is a specific time at night set by local law when juveniles are not allowed out of their home without adult supervision or for an emergency.

Some reasons that juveniles are apprehended are extremely vague. Two examples are being ungovernable and in need of supervision.

Juvenile law, in various sates apprehend juveniles for non-criminal offenses under various labels:

- MINS   Minors in Need of Supervision
- FINS   Families in Need of Supervision
- PINS   Persons in Need of Supervision
- YINS   Youths in Need of Supervision
- CHINS   Children in Need of Supervision.

To keep this simple, we will use the term *delinquents* for juveniles who have committed an act that would be a crime if the juveniles were adults. We will use person in need of supervision, or *PINS*, for juveniles who have committed a status offense that would not be a criminal offense for adults.

Youths may be referred to the juvenile justice system by many different sources such as neighbors, social service agencies, private businesses, the schools, the police as well as parents and other legal guardians. To make the system come alive for the reader, we have introduced three typical case histories that happen all over America. The following are typical examples illustrating how juveniles may come into the justice system.

Three Case Histories For Intake

First Case History: A Status Offense

A juvenile breaks a neighbor's window with a baseball and the neighbors call the police. If the parents are not available, the juvenile is brought to the police station and then referred to probation. If the parents are available, the police normally let the neighbors and the parents work it out informally, if possible.

The Intake Unit of Probation would normally receive this case where the probation officer would attempt to successfully deal with the case at this level to prevent the case from going to juvenile court. In some jurisdictions, this is called the Intake/Diversion Unit.

Some probation agencies may offer a mediation service that would keep the juvenile out of the justice system. **Mediation** is a process where the juvenile and the people complaining about the juvenile's behavior resolve their problems to everyone's satisfaction, with the help of a third party called a mediator. In this example, the mediator would be a probation officer unless the case is sent to a mediating agency.

If mediation does not work, the neighbor can submit a formal petition to juvenile court. The neighbor does this by filing a juvenile court petition. The court would set a hearing date and decide at the hearing what to do about the situation.

If the juvenile judge decided that the juvenile did break the neighbor's window, the judge could order the juvenile to pay to fix the window. The juvenile could also admit to the judge that he broke the window. The juvenile is seen to be responsible for his or her actions rather than the parents or guardians. It is then up to the juvenile to repair the window rather than having the parents or guardians pay for the window. The judge would most likely put the juvenile on probation for a specific period of time and order other conditions and penalties. Professionals in juvenile justice would say that the judge could "attach" other conditions and penalties. After going through juvenile court, the juvenile is now in the juvenile justice system.

Second Case History: A Criminal Offense

A juvenile burglarizes an empty camp during MISSING TEXT and the police arrest him in the act. The juvenile is read his rights and brought to the police station where he may be fingerprinted. His parents or guardians are immediately notified. The youth is usually held in detention or put into his parents' or guardians' custody until a court appearance. No bail is legally available for juveniles. The juvenile remains under the jurisdiction of the court until a juvenile court judge makes a decision at a formal hearing.

The police would do an investigation of the burglary to see what was stolen or damaged and if there were other juveniles or adults involved in the crime. An attorney often known as a law guardian would be appointed by the court to defend the interests of the juvenile at public expense. A probation officer would interview the youth and do an extensive social history. The juvenile would appear in court and most likely admit he did the burglary since he was caught at the scene of the crime but he could also say he did not do it. This is called agreeing to the facts of the burglary or denying the facts of the burglary. He could be adjudicated as a juvenile delinquent and formally placed on probation or institutionalized. This is a formal procedure of due process for juvenile court.

Third Case History: A Status Offense

Another example is when a juvenile does not commit a crime but engages in behavior that has been made illegal for juveniles but is not illegal for adults.

A juvenile, age thirteen, runs away from home and the frantic parents notify the police about their missing child. The child is spotted with her friends drinking a beer at midnight on a street corner. The police pick up the child and the parents are notified.

The police may simply return the child to the parents and recommend counseling. The juvenile justice system is not involved even though running away from home and drinking beer are juvenile offenses. If the parents or guardians are not available the police may have to place the child in detention until the parents or guardians are found. The police could also ask the juvenile court and probation to intervene. A child abuse and/or neglect investigation may be initiated, depending on why the juvenile ran away from home and any suspicious circumstances. At this point the juvenile has entered the system.

Best Interest of the Child Principle

What normally brings a juvenile into the system is the juveniles' violation of specific juvenile justice or school laws. The juvenile courts have also established jurisdiction and authority over a child using the "best interest of the child" principle. Parents who abuse or neglect their children come under the juvenile courts' jurisdiction. The court may provide social services or even take the child out of Abuse and Neglect homes.

The juveniles may not be at fault but they are still in the system. They may be placed outside of their home usually in some kind of foster care. Social services may intervene in their home by providing some kind of family counseling. The reason for this is that government agencies and the courts may feel that the juveniles may come to some *harm*. These are called "**at risk**" juveniles in the language of social services.

Children and Adolescents As Victims of Neglect and Abuse

Neglect and Abuse cases are brought against adults for victimizing children and adolescents. The effect is often to bring children and adolescents in to the juvenile justice and social service systems when they are taken from their homes.

Children and adolescents are endangered most often with physical assault including being beaten up and sexual victimization. Psychological, mental or emotional harm examples are hard to prove without any physical evidence. Standardized psychological tests and psychological evaluations by professionals are often used in evidence. Neglect includes not being housed adequately, fed or

15

clothed. Neglect also includes being kept from going to school, and lack of proper medical care.

Unintentional harm can be caused by ignorance of how to care for a child. One example is a single mother who was mentally retarded. Her baby was having sores because the baby's diaper was not being changed for a number of days. A public health nurse was sent in to teach the mother how to take care of the child. The mother, with supervision, was able to eventually raise the baby in her home.

Some juveniles come into the system because their parents cannot control them. The juvenile may threaten the parents in the home or use foul language continually. They may leave the home at all times of the day and night without the parents' permission and bring alcohol and drugs into the home. Parents may worry about their own safety and their other children's safety in the home. The parents can file a petition with juvenile court and ask for help.

Juveniles come in the system through four major ways:

1. By being victimized by their parents or guardians through neglect and abuse statutes when they are taken out of the home,
2. By violating a criminal law and/or being arrested by the police,
3. By violating a juvenile offense that is not an adult crime, such as running away from home or not attending public school,
4. By being petitioned into the system by their parents, guardians and public or private institutions.

Information Collecting

Great care is taken to find out if a juvenile should be referred to the justice system. Information is collected at two places in the process:

1. At Probation Intake, the beginning of the process before the juvenile goes to court and

2. After the court appearance and before disposition. This information is also used for placing the individual into group homes, foster care, incarceration, and probation, etc.

This collection of information in a Social History at the start of the process becomes part of the predisposition report for juvenile sentencing. A probation officer will interview the parents and/or guardians, the juvenile, victims, and any one else involved.

The predisposition report, which is requested by the court, is similar to a presentence report in the adult system with some real differences. The predisposition report emphasis is on treatment and community integration. In contrast the adult presentence report emphasis is usually on equitable punishment called just desserts.

The first step in the Social History is to identify past behaviors and experiences of the juvenile. The juvenile's motivation and capacity for treatment is evaluated. A description of the juvenile's home and family is crucial. What kind of help will be best for the juvenile given the juvenile's capacity for self-direction is evaluated. It also includes social opportunities that are available as well as the indicators of future goals and treatment.

Elements Of The Social History

We will use the term Social History as the label for collecting data and to assess the data on individual youths. It is a report requested by the court. A petition/complaint is a legal document, which tells the juvenile judge why the juvenile should be in court. The predisposition report has more detail because it is making recommendations from probation to the judge concerning the potential disposition of the juvenile. The predisposition report is the basis for placing the juvenile in different programs, including intuitions, foster care, alcohol and drug abuse programs, etc., or sending the juvenile home. The needs and risk assessments would only include part of the social history.

The Social History has a number of specific elements that are important to know about for everyone involved in the juvenile justice system including: parents or guardians, juveniles, lawyers, counselors and mental health professionals, youth workers, social workers, judges and probation officers to name just the main participants. Each element of the Social History is verified and analyzed for its effect on the juvenile and the juvenile's ultimate disposition. The Social History will follow the juvenile throughout the juvenile justice system.

The Social History is the basic data and analysis used for the need assessment and the risk assessment. The need assessment documents what services a youth may need. For example, drug counseling, a tutor for school or a new home or placement. The risk assessment shows how much of a threat the delinquent is to the community. The risk assessment will determine if the youth is to be in a secure placement or a nonsecure placement in the community.

It is important that the accuracy of the statements and facts in the social history be verified and as accurate as possible. It is the duty of any person who uses the social history to correct any errors.

The Offense

The elements included in the Social History start with the crime or behavior that brought the juvenile into the justice system. The probation officer interviewing the juvenile usually does this. The officer also examines all the legal documents provided by the police and the courts. This would include specifics of a criminal history.

The information needed is the date, description of the offense, and type of offense, e.g. from running away to burglary. It is especially important to document the seriousness of the offense since this will have a major impact on what the court will decide to do with the juvenile.

Most juveniles engage in crimes with their friends. So the offense description has to show what role others had in the offense. These can be codefendants, accessories or even witnesses.

History

This includes family history, individual personal history and legal history. The family history would include geographic moves, job changes, brothers and sisters, divorces and separations, stepparents and the general changing history of the family including court and social services interventions. The personal history would follow the youth from birth to the present including school changes and living circumstances. The legal history would include any trouble with the law in any jurisdiction.

The Family

The juvenile's immediate family has a profound effect on a juvenile's behavior and life style. The most important questions concern the economic and emotional stability and resources of parents, guardians and anyone who lives with the family. Since supervision of juveniles is a major need in terms of juvenile success, this will be closely analyzed.

The major problems that show up in the social history are:

- Drug and alcohol abuse
- Family violence
- Emotional abuse
- Lack of supervision
- Effect of criminal neighborhoods
- Poor school attendance and grades.

Delinquent parents and guardians may display inconsistent discipline. If these adults punish and reward behavior at random, their children never have a chance to learn right from wrong (Thomas, 1970; Wilson and Herrnstein, 1985).

Children of poor, single parents living in criminal neighborhoods with little or no supervision, have the highest risk for delinquency. Children of middle class single parents living in good neighborhoods have a low risk of delinquency. Two-parent emotionally stable families also have lower risks. (Wright and Wright, 1995)

Personality Traits
(Siegel, Welsh and Senna: 94–99, 2006)

Serious delinquents, generally lack emotional stability and middle class moral values. Boys tend to be more aggressive while girls tend toward promiscuous and suicidal behavior. Various standardized tests are used along with interviews with professionals in mental health. Delinquents compared to youth who do not get into trouble, are more likely to be egocentric, impulsive, with low anger control and poor social skills. They also lack empathy, which is the ability to put yourself in the place of another and really feel their pain. Without empathy, they could hurt a person and be indifferent to their pain. Siegel, Welsh and Senna, 2006: 94–95.

A major trait of delinquents is immediate gratification. Delinquents are hasty hedonists. They want it all "NOW!" and usually do not sacrifice present pleasures for future rewards. Middle class students go to school in order to have a better future and a good career. A delinquent will steal a car rather than work for it. Delinquents generally do not feel guilty for their actions since they lack strong middle class feelings of right from wrong.

Male delinquents are aggressive while female delinquents, in the past, have been more suicidal. This has been changing rapidly with many female delinquents having mostly the same traits as male delinquents. Occasional delinquents lack most of these delinquent traits and often become good citizens. Serious delinquents have a pattern of these traits and get into serious trouble.

The Diagnostic and Statistical Manual of the America Psychiatric Association (DSM) describes psychotic and neurotic behaviors that are formally diagnosed with counseling that may be paid for by insurance. The DSM, as it is referred to, has a section on conduct disorder for mentally ill juveniles. Conduct disorder is a general description of some delinquent behaviors used by mental health professionals to diagnose troubled youth.

Peers and Friendships

These refer to close personal friends of the delinquent youth. Most delinquents are adolescents and adolescents are greatly influenced by their friends and teen-age culture. They hang out with their friends. They do drugs, sex, alcohol and crime with their friends as well as conventional activities.

Becoming a member of a gang is the most serious of criminal behaviors for a delinquent. Knowing an influential middle class friend can help an occasional delinquent to change behaviors, which may lead to a conventional life style. (Inciardi, Horowitz and Pottieger. 1995.)

School

Adolescents spend a good deal of time in school and success in school is important to them. Staying and succeeding in school is crucial to successful intervention with delinquents. A school solution to an adolescent troublemaker or drug dealer is to suspend or expel them so they have more time for their street business. The research shows that the girls have time to trade sex for drugs while the boys have more time to become full time crack dealers. (Inciardi, Horowitz and Pottieger. 1995.) Alternate schools have been successful for intervention in delinquent life styles but in general the public schools have failed the delinquent population.

A Social History needs to document school attendance, grades, educational assessment scores, social adjustments, and interviews with teachers, vice-principals and school counselors. Students are at risk when they socially isolated or become involved with a marginal group of students.

Drugs and Alcohol Abuse

The earlier in age drug and alcohol abuse is started the longer the addictions and the more negative the effects, especially if it starts in the home. Children of abusers and children who are not supervised are at greater risk. Adolescent drug and alcohol parties, often without the knowledge of parents, irrespective of social class, leads to risky sexual behavior and delinquency. It is essential that this abuse be documented since much of this behavior is hidden from responsible adults. Adolescents who become drug pushers are most often multiple drug users and have a pattern of petty crimes to feed their habit.

Medical History Including Emotional and Physical Disability

This is especially important for the needs assessments since this will determine medications, medical help and disability accommodations in housing. Any persistent problems like diabetes or asthma are essential to know for placement and care. Part of a solution to bad grades may be as simple as new eyeglasses, better contrast in letters or a change in medicines. A history of depression or other mental illness may help explain behaviors. Allergies to foods need to be documented. Problems may be resolved by dealing medically with a disfigurement. A different and balanced diet with less sugar and the right vitamins does wonders with some adolescent behavior.

Conclusion to the Social History

The Social History is the basic document that all juvenile justice decisions are based upon. Professionals who have never seen or talked to a troubled youth will make decisions based on the Social History. A judge will use the Social History to make a decision, which will surely change this youth's life, forever. An administrator in a youth's home will make a decision to admit a youth to a home or special counseling program based on the social history. In a large juvenile justice organization, youths' lives become summarized and evaluated through the Social History.

The Assessment Model

The purpose for collecting the Social History information is to evaluate the juvenile and the juvenile behavior.

The assessment model evaluates the juvenile's total conduct:

- **Risk to the community**—how dangerous or violent the juveniles are.
- **Needs**—what does the juvenile need to succeed in life?
- **Strengths**—what positive personal strengths does the juvenile have?
- **Accountability for his or her behavior**—this stresses the juvenile's responsibility and subsequent accountability for any harm done to individuals and the community. The juvenile then becomes responsible for restoring any harm done.

Professionals use the information in the Social History to create assessment documents for the court and other government agencies such as petition and predisposition reports, along with the risk assessment and needs already mentioned. The assessments are then used to determine what will be done with the juvenile; for example, to institutionalize a juvenile or place the juvenile on probation.

The assessments are used to decide upon:

1. The disposition and placement of the juvenile
2. Professional evaluations of the juvenile
3. The basis for providing services
4. Protecting the community

We will use Social History as a generic term and refer to its various uses where appropriate.

Petition Assessment and Diversion

The Petition Assessment is a brief document used by Probation to assess the needs, risks and placement of a juvenile when the juvenile first comes into the system. It is like a Social History without the detail. The probation officer needs to decide if this youth needs to go to court or if the probation department can take care of the case at the intake level. It is also used for diverting juveniles from the juvenile justice system into community service and other community programs. Typical behaviors for these cases are vandalism, shoplifting, skipping school, and fighting. Diversion provides services and supervision of short duration for both juveniles and their families.

Diversion is a process where juvenile delinquents and persons in need of supervision are "diverted" or moved away from the juvenile justice formal system.

They are usually moved to a community-based agency or assigned to a youth counselor for social and psychiatric assistance.

A diversion program's underlying philosophy is community integration and rehabilitation. This may include job training, special education programs and psychological counseling. Two major criteria for selecting a juvenile for this approach are normally a first time offender and petty offenses rather than major crimes. Participants in diversion programs usually participate for shorter periods of time such as a few weeks or months rather than long term counseling. These short periods of time can be stipulated by legislation depending on the type of diversion program and jurisdiction. The programs vary widely around the country and even from county to county.

Lawyers

The US Supreme Court has decided that juveniles have the right to a lawyer. The court-appointed lawyer, also called a law guardian, represents the juvenile and does not represent the parents or the family in any way. Parents need to be concerned that this court-appointed lawyer has some experience in juvenile courts and understands the language and rules of the juvenile court. They should be concerned that this lawyer knows the details of their child's case. If these two factors are not in place, the parents need to talk to the juvenile judge about their concerns.

Some parents hire a private lawyer. There is a dispute whether a private lawyer hired by parents can even represent a child since the parents are paying the lawyer's fees. Judges have appointed lawyers to represent the child even though the family has provided a lawyer for the child.

If parents hire a lawyer, they need to interview the lawyer and ask some professional and billing questions. Billing is when a lawyer bills the parents for the lawyer's time and expense. In hiring a lawyer ask him or her the following questions. You can read them from this book:

Hiring A Private Lawyer

—Some lawyers don't charge for an initial interview and some do. Ask if an initial appointment is free. If it is not free, ask what the fee for this initial meeting will be. If a fee is charged, the client should expect an analysis of the case, as the lawyer understands the issues.

—Ask: How much do you charge per hour? Ask, if there is a smaller hourly fee for secretarial time and a paralegal's time. Find out if there is a higher hourly fee for time spent in court before a judge. Does the lawyer want a down payment on the bill called a retainer fee? Feel free to ask approximately what the total cost might be. Ask around to find out what most lawyers in juvenile court charge for their time.

—See if you will be charged for 1/10 of an hour, 1/4 of an hour, 1/2 an hour or a full hourly rate including any part of an hour. If you phone and talk for ten minutes and the lawyer charges $300 an hour, will that ten minutes cost you 1/10 of $300 or $30 dollars or 1/2 of an hour for $150 dollars?

—Ask the lawyer: How long have you practiced in the juvenile justice system and approximately how many cases have you handled?

—If possible, describe the case in writing concerning your child with all the facts and any legal documents like an arrest report. Let the lawyer read these materials. Remember the more organized you are, the better chance for success and the less time the lawyer needs to spend on the case at these high hourly rates.

—Show the lawyer the arrest report and ask, "How serious are the charges?"

—Ask the lawyer what may happen next to your child.

—Listen to the lawyer's advice and only hire the lawyer if you feel this advice and information is worth the money. The lawyer is an officer of the court. You can always hire another lawyer.

Always go to court when there is a hearing even if your lawyer says there is no need to go or that it is routine. Serious decisions are made in court and before you know it, you and your children will have little or no part in the decision. Be involved and always show up at all court appearances. Be informed and ask questions. This advice applies to the juveniles involved and all professionals involved.

Conclusion

The purpose of this chapter has been to describe in clear English how the intake system works and how it affects juveniles, their parents and guardians. It is our intent that professionals, parents and juveniles have a clear understanding of the juvenile justice system.

This is an introduction to how juveniles become involved in the juvenile justice system. The intake process is primarily a series of decisions made by a probation officer who handles the case. As discussed before, the juvenile comes to the attention of Probation through many procedures and referrals such as schools, parents or an arresting officer.

The following decisions are made concerning the juvenile:

- Is this a case for intake services or should the juvenile be immediately referred to Juvenile Court? The first decision means the juvenile will be in the system for a limited time and the case will be handled more informally. The second part of the decision means that the behavior is more serious and will be handled formally through the court system. The parents' cooperation is crucial to making this decision.

- Does any action need to be taken or can the family handle the situation on an informal basis? If the family can take care of the situation, the intake probation officer will meet with the family and refer the juvenile back to the family. This means the juvenile is out of the system.

- Is there some community resource, which can handle the problem immediately? If a resource is available, the intake officer makes the referral and the juvenile is out of the system. For example, if there were an alcohol problem, an adolescent alcoholic counseling program would be a good referral.

- If the case is held at intake, can a brief service solve the problem? An intake probation officer could counsel the juvenile for a brief period, and then the juvenile is out of the system.

This is the beginning of the process. Later sections of this *Guidebook* will describe other treatments and the formal processing through the juvenile system.

Laypersons who are not professionally part of the juvenile justice system need to pay attention to the details of the Social History and the various assessment reports. They need to obtain copies of these documents and any arrest reports created by the system because they can have a profound effect on a juvenile's life.

The Juvenile Justice System And The Family

Chapter Outline

Introduction

Juvenile delinquents and "persons in need of supervision" do not live in a vacuum. Their antisocial behavior comes, in good part, from external forces. The family is the primary source of proper behavior and values in the rearing of children.

When an adolescent is arrested, many parents or guardians blame the adolescent's friends, television or violent video games. There may be some truth to this but the family and the adolescent are primarily responsible for the antisocial behavior. Many parents are in what is called denial concerning the reality of the arrest and its consequences. The burden of dealing with the juvenile justice system is the responsibility of the family. The parents or guardians have to accept this responsibility so that the adolescent can learn and benefit from this experience.

Family issues are repeated for every generation. In 1978, Onondaga County Probation developed a "Family Crisis Intervention" paper and unit. The recommendations on the first page are specific and relevant to today's families with troubled children.

> "... the patterns of poor communication, ill defined roles and inadequate problem solving methods are reinforced by the increased tension of anticipating and participation in court sessions. Clearly what is needed is a method for intervening with the family of such children and concentrate efforts to (1) relieve the immediate tension, (2) discover the underlying reason for malfunction of the family and, (3) incorporate methods to break a pattern of repeated dysfunction." (Onondaga Probation, 1978: 1)

Troubled children who become involved with the law usually mean a troubled family. During this same decade, Morton Bard in New York City was creating a New York City Police Department family crisis intervention unit, which became a successful model for the nation. Family issues haven't really changed and the focus is still on the family.

The juvenile justice system should not be viewed as the primary agency responsible for changing antisocial behavior. All children need a family, a school, recreation, food, clothing and shelter. However, all children do not need juvenile court. Juveniles grow up in the family and will come back to the family from the justice system. The Juvenile Justice System may prevent some juvenile delinquency. The prevention of the initial delinquency is basically the job of the family. Other community sources come into play but the family is primarily responsible for raising children.

The 21st Century American Family

1. Extended Kinship Family: Mainly related by blood and marriage. This type of family has existed for centuries and is a significant structure for rural and immigrant families. For example, Mexican immigrants in the United States send millions of dollars to extended family members in Mexico. Juveniles in extended families are nurtured by grandparents, aunts, uncles, siblings and cousins.

2. Cluster Family in lower class neighborhood. This type of family operates much like the extended family with relatives, neighbors and friends forming relationships to help each other out, deal with government regulations and agents, raise the children and supervise the adolescents in the family.

3. Nuclear Family: Mom, Dad and the children. This is a relatively socially isolated family with much geographic mobility, living in middle class neighborhoods and the suburbs. Babysitters, daycare and schools take the place of the extended family.

4. The Single Parent Family is composed mostly of Single Mother Families. Since the divorces, separation and custody system favors mothers over fathers in court-ordered custody decisions, the United States generally has over 85% single parent families who are mothers raising adolescents and children. These families drop in economic social class after separation and divorce and generally do not have the resources to provide adequate supervision for adolescents, once again, in their most vulnerable years. (Rice, 1996, Straus and Gelles, 1990, Ricci, 1980, U.S. Census web sites)

5. Step Family, also call the Merged Family: usually is a mother with her biological children and a stepfather with none of his biological children living with him. Although this family has more supervision than the single parent family, a major problem for adolescents is competition of authority between the biological

31

mother and the stepfather. The stepfather often has less authority with the children. Both parents need to have consistency and back each other when asserting authority over an adolescent's behavior. Overall, adopted children do as well as biological related children and their families. (Ricci, 1980, U.S. Census web sites, any sociological book on the family)

Note: These family structures overlap because the reality of their lives overlap. Children and adolescents grow up in these family structures, every day.

The following are from U.S. Census Web Sites:

From 1970–2002, single mother families grew from 3 million to ten million and single father families from 393,00 to 3 million. In 2002, 16.5 million children under the age of 18 lived with single mothers and 3.3 million with single fathers. Dad's unmarried partner lived in 1.1 million of these households and mom's unmarried partner lived in 1.8 million of the single mother households. This is a growing problem that is producing troubled and delinquent children and little is being done to stop the decline of the two-parent family in sheer numbers. In 1960, 80.6% of children lived in two-parent households. This has declined to 68% two-parent households in 2002.

In the year 2000, 74% of white children and 64% of Spanish speaking household children lived with two parents. Only 36% of African American children lived with two parents. In 2002 about one out of three children in the United States did not live with two parents. As reported over the years, of those living in single mother households, over one third had not seen their father for a year.

America has the largest percentage of children living in one-parent families in the industrialized world. The United States is engaged in a major social experiment of raising a large percent of several generations of children without their fathers and for a smaller number, without their mothers. For lower class children, the resulting lack of supervision and disruption of family life has proved to be a major disaster. Today a majority of women in America are not married and almost that high a percentage of men are not married. (The figures on the make-up of the American family come from the U.S. Census Bureau.)

In 2003 two new trends emerged with a decrease in teen pregnancies and an increase in married households as reported in the U.S. Census publication *American Families Living Arrangements* (Fields, 2004).

"The decades-long decline in the proportion of family groups with children that were married-couple families leveled off during the mid-1990s, at about 68 percent from 1996 to 2003 (Figure 1). This change reflects declining divorce rates and reduced non-marital fertility, especially among teens. Between 1970 and 1996, the median age at first marriage also increased but since 1996 has been fairly stable for both men and women."

Most Delinquents Come From Lower Class Families

The following lower class family characteristics has been collected from many family and stratification textbooks over many years.

- More open to sexual expression.
- Fewer resources for pregnant women and their children.
- Older brothers and sisters more engaged in child rearing with less time for childhood and adolescence.
- Feeling crowded in more restrictive quarters increases stress of everyday living.
- Birth of children is used to set up independent households funded by welfare for females.
- Fathers have marginal incomes with no benefits. Mothers have marginal incomes from welfare, with benefits for themselves and their children.
- Social Services dependency is created and sustained.

- Less health resources, poor starchy diets and almost no dental services
- Poor schools and more violence in schools resulting in less life chances for success
- High drug and alcohol use
- No middle class achievement orientation
- High unemployment and minimum wage provides the working poor with marginal jobs. Middle class people have careers; lower class people have dead end jobs
- High-risk neighborhoods dominated by single mothers and unemployed, rogue males

Family Life and Delinquency: Conclusions From The Research

(Wright and Wright, 1995, a brilliant summary of the research)

The Single Mother: less than 1% of single mother white families live in poverty. Minority single mothers chiefly live in poverty. Roughly one out of four families in America have a single mother as head of household. In many poor black neighborhoods the ration is four out of five with a single mother household

Poverty, a tough neighborhood, lack of supervision from a single mother and a large number of high-risk males leads to delinquency. As long as this persists, delinquency will be concentrated in these families and neighborhoods. Most children including those growing up with single mothers are not delinquents

Attachment and bonding to conventional parents with working class and middle class values reduces the risk of delinquency. This includes a family environment of affection, cohesion, involvement and supervision. Parental rejection is a significant predictor of delinquency. Marital discord is consistently related to delinquency. Child neglect and abuse is clearly related to delinquency.

Parents play a critical role in the moral development of children and adolescents. Especially critical is developing an appreciation of the relationship between behavior and consequences and the development of empathy. The lack of family supervision is closely linked to delinquency. Positive parenting combined with the continual parental involvement with their children protect children from becoming delinquent.

Parenting Styles and Juvenile Delinquency
(Wilson and Herrnstein, 1985)

1. Warm Restrictive These children and youth will respect and internalize middle class values, seek out and appreciate the approval of adults and follow middle class norms in their behavior. They will have the needed boundaries in their lives to feel safe while knowing that they are loved.

2. Warm Permissive These children and youths will be open, social and self-confident. They will be pleasant to be around and appear to be law abiding. However, they will also be manipulative, seeking ways to go around middle class rules and beat the system.

3. Cold Restrictive The parents will be overly strict without warm feelings toward their children. These children and youths will obey the middle class rules but will have strong feeling of anger, which may translate into rebellion. Anger turned inward may result in suicidal behavior and depression. Anger turned outward may result in bursts of violence,

| | violation of the middle class norms and rebellion leading to delinquency. |
| **4. Cold Permissive** | These children and youths are at the highest risk for delinquency having no boundaries to their lives or adherence to middle class norms while being angry at the rejection and indifference of their parents. |

Warm restrictive parenting with a consistent set of rules is the parenting style most likely to have happy children and youths who will respect and obey middle class norms. When parents, schools and/or the courts are *inconsistent* in applying rules, children and youths quickly learn that there is no relationship between their behavior and the consequences of behavior. In other words, punishment for bad behavior and rewards for good behavior is random. Adolescents will feel free to be larcenous, aggressive and violent because rewards and punishments have nothing to do with behavior. With no consequences to behavior, children and adolescents will feel they can do anything they want. Punishment will have no consistent relation to his or her behavior. Children understand swift, sure and consistent punishment. Random punishment, not related to behavior, undermines a sense of justice and fair play.

Involvement of the Family

If your son or daughter has never been arrested, the arrest comes as a shock to everyone in the family. Everyone is upset and is wondering what to do. What the family has to do is to take this seriously and deal with it.

The first thing to do is find out what happened. Talk to the juvenile and get a copy of the arrest report to find out the facts. The family may need a lawyer. Call family and friends to see if they know a lawyer who has practiced in the juvenile system. A civil lawyer who draws up business and real estate contracts will not do because that lawyer does not know how the specialized juvenile court works. The family needs somebody familiar with the juvenile justice system and the relevant laws and cases. The Juvenile Justice System can be very different from the adult justice system.

As mentioned before, the court will most likely appoint a lawyer to represent the juvenile. The family may also wish to hire a private lawyer to represent the family interests. What you should consider in hiring a lawyer is covered in chapter one.

The family needs to have a support group of friends and family to talk to and lean on emotionally. Dealing with the Juvenile Justice System may take a few days, months and sometimes years. Family members need to prepare themselves and work through this crisis. Life needs to go on. Family members need to go to work, get enough sleep and eat healthy meals and take care of each other.

The Juvenile Justice System is a large government organization and the family is really going to need expert help here. The juvenile may be sitting in jail and needs that family support system and good advice. The juvenile will also be coming home and will have to go to school and make up back school work. It is important that the home be a safe place, emotionally and physically, for the juvenile to come home to.

The family may want to hire or seek out professional counseling for themselves and their children. Probation officers, social workers and juvenile workers can be helpful and a good place to seek advice. The parents know there is a reason their child is in trouble and the family has to do something about it.

Once the juvenile is adjudicated, the juvenile will be under the jurisdiction of the court. The judge will decide based on such factors as age and the type of offense. For example, Joey, age 15 skips school for a month making him legally truant. Joey then comes under the jurisdiction of a juvenile court as an adjudicated Person In Need of Supervision (PINS). Joey could also steal a car, which is a crime, and come under the court's jurisdiction as a delinquent.

Under the rule of "Parens Patria" the government may become the legal guardian of the child. If this happens, the courts and the juvenile justice system will be in charge of the child's life. Parents would have to be proven to be "unfit parents" in court. This happens when parents neglect their children by not providing adequate food, clothing, shelter or education (going to school). Parents can be unfit by abusing their child with violence or sexual assault. The courts are very reluctant to take away parental rights. With good and sufficient reason, this can happen and will involve extensive investigation by the government. Parental rights can be restored but it will be a long, costly and tough process.

The juvenile justice judges have many options ranging from taking a juvenile out of the home to placing the juvenile on probation or even dismissing the case. All these decisions will demand a good deal of involvement with the family.

Probation Intake has the option to use non-judicial means to deal with these juveniles. This means juveniles do not have to go to a formal hearing in family court. The courts like this because fewer juveniles come before juvenile court. The courts can then have more time to deal with more serious matters such as criminal offenses. Other dispositions would be probation supervision, commitment to secure and non-secure institutions such as group homes, foster care. Community-based agencies, both public and private, provide a wide variety of services to the juvenile and the juvenile's family.

The juvenile court system imposes a legal responsibility on parents and guardians to assume and maintain a continuous participation with their children through all phases and dispositions of the juvenile justice system. For example, parents and guardians may need to participate in counseling services involving their children. This family involvement is from the first contact with the juvenile system with only probation supervision all the way to having a juvenile released from an institution. When juveniles are placed in a group home, for example, parents and guardians often have visiting time and juveniles may come home for some weekends. Many juveniles are released to the parents' home while the juvenile is under the court's supervision. Probation officers and social service workers may make home visitations. There are hundreds of examples available.

Coming Home: Role of the Family

What is important, in most cases, is that the family stays involved and supportive. In almost every case, the juveniles come home. They come home from foster care, jails, group homes and juvenile institutions many hundreds of miles away from the parents' home. They come home looking for their family's love and support. Both the family and the juveniles may have a chance to grow. After all, these adolescents, in a few short years, will have their own homes and families.

The parents or guardians have to provide boundaries and restrictions on the juveniles while providing a loving home. Juveniles may have court-ordered and probation restrictions such as curfews, staying away from criminal friends, drugs and alcohol. Going to drug and alcohol counseling and programs with evidence of attendance is a normal part of probation services. Coming home from school and doing homework before playing sports or video games may be some rules imposed by probation.

Adolescents are very social but restrictions along with warm loving support have to become part of family life. This is how the warm, restrictive parental style is applied. It works when the parents or guardians take responsibility for family life and most of all are consistent. Parents need to keep their word to juveniles in a consistent manner while juveniles need to learn to keep their word to their parents. Adolescents feel more secure and loved in their own home when there are reasonable and consistent boundaries placed on their behavior.

CHAPTER

3

Diversion, Juvenile Agencies And Community-Based Services

Chapter Outline

Introduction

How social agencies handle a juvenile has a major impact on the adolescent and his or her family. Following is a general description of each juvenile agency and the services each can provide for the juvenile and his or her family. The juvenile could be involved in many of these agencies well before any juvenile court appearance. Working with these agencies can provide families and youths with solutions to many personal and social problems.

Social services and school social workers and counselors could be working with the juvenile and his family; a private agency could be providing services through a neighborhood youth program. Probation has many programs to help adolescents work out the problems in their life and keep troubled youths from getting involved with the juvenile court system. Later in this Juvenile Justice Guide, we will explain in specific detail what happens when a youth goes to court. At this point rather than involving the juvenile in official court dispositions and procedures, let us take a look at how juveniles can be **diverted** from the courts.

How Diversion Works

Diversion has had a long history in juvenile justice. A few juveniles, roughly 5–7%, have committed serious crimes (Inciardi, Horowitz, Pottieger, 1993). Over 90% of juveniles come into the system for less serious offenses such as curfew violation, shoplifting, running away from home and truancy from school. Best practice by juvenile justice professionals is to lessen the impact of the justice system on these less troubled youths and their families whenever possible.

Diversion also saves our tax dollars by not spending tax money on services that are not needed, When diversion is applied, it stops the penetration of juveniles into the formal justice system. "Widening the net" is a criticism of diversion that states that juveniles who should not be in the system are brought into the system by the informal process of diversion. Diversion should do just the opposite. Fewer juveniles would be brought into the formal justice system because of the presence of diversion programs and policies.

The first rule, of course, is to do no harm. It would be harming these juveniles and be a waste of services to bring these youths further into the system more than is needed to deal with their problems. Since these are still youths under eighteen, the professionals in the juvenile justice system would rather *not* take these children from their families and local neighborhoods. The research over the years supports a family-based counseling approach for most troubled youths.

Under diversion policies for most juveniles the following approaches would apply:

- Leave the youth with his or her family.
- Provide counseling services to the youth and the family to help them deal with immediate problems over a short period of time.
- Use diversion programs to provide these services before there is a need for juvenile court intervention.
- Diversion programs should be based in the juvenile home community.

Probation Agencies: Intake and Diversion

The juvenile first comes into contact with probation and the formal juvenile justice system at **Probation Intake.** Referrals to probation come from law enforcement, school, parents or citizens such as neighbors. The probation officer at juvenile intake determines whether a juvenile case should be handled informally or referred to juvenile court. This decision is based on social and legal factors, the seriousness of the offense and a youth's offense history. It makes a big difference if this was the first offense or a tenth offense and whether it was for running away or burglary. However, intake /diversion may entail a short appearance before a judge in juvenile court where the juvenile is referred to probation so that probation can provide intake services.

The probation officer decides from the facts presented by the persons making the referral to probation and other sources of information, whether the youth committed the offense. If the officer decides the youth committed the offense, then in order to qualify for services, at this stage, the youth must admit to wrongdoing. The juvenile must also agree to specific conditions of behavior such as attending school, restitution and/or a curfew. If the youth denies that he or she committed the offense, the matter will usually be referred to juvenile court.

If the juvenile meets all conditions of this informal supervision at intake over a period of time anywhere from a few days to a few months, the case is dismissed. Violating these conditions of probation may lead to a formal referral to juvenile court. An example of violation behavior would be if the juvenile were given a curfew to be at home at seven P.M. at night. The juvenile may be recorded as staying out past midnight for many nights. With this record of violating the probation conditions, probation may refer the case to the court for a violation hearing. A new crime will also result in a formal violation hearing.

Probation departments provide a wide variety of service to troubled juveniles and their families in cooperation with social services, mental health agencies and other public and private agencies. At the intake stage, probation hopes to divert the juvenile from becoming more formally involved in the juvenile court system. Most of the time this works with most juveniles and these juveniles go back to their homes to lead normal lives without getting into trouble with the criminal law. Limited services and supervision provided over a brief period of time generally do a fine job for most juveniles.

If there is a need for more extensive services, probation will bring the youth through the court system in order to get court-ordered services. The court, working closely with probation, may refer the juvenile to a public or a private agency for placement and for services.

> **Case Study:** Initially the youth, for example, may have a minor alcoholic drinking problem. Further investigation shows a great deal of alcohol abuse. The youth is then sent for an alcoholic evaluation and the findings indicate that alcohol abuse is a major problem for this youth. The youth's family may have insurance or the money needed to provide privates services, which can be very expensive. If alcohol abuse services are not financially affordable by the family, the court may order services provided by the city, county or state. If the juvenile alcoholic hangs out with alcoholic friends, it may be necessary to place the youth in an institution outside of the home. The level of services is determined by the seriousness of the problem.

Juvenile and Family Counseling

What services are provided is determined by the extent of both the individual juvenile problems and family problems. A lower class family living in a poor neighborhood may need extensive services with financial and personal counseling from a variety of agencies. The family may be already receiving services from a variety of agencies. Normally, the juvenile may be one person in a family with many problems. Probation will then need to coordinate services for the youth and family with a variety of agencies and should be prepared to do so.

A middle class family in a stable neighborhood may need some help providing adequate supervision. Some youths use drugs and alcohol in their local school while lying to their parents about their behavior. (Wooden, 2001) Intervention by a professional probation officer can alert the family to these problems and show them where adequate counseling services can be provided. Adolescents who live a great deal of their life without adequate supervision by professional "busy" parents can be at great risk for multiproblem behaviors. The solution in these cases is raising the parents' consciousness of what is going on in their troubled children's lives and what services and family solutions are available.

Restitution

Restitution means that juvenile delinquents take the responsibility to compensate victims and restore communities that have been damaged. Restore means to fix the damage done. If a juvenile, for example, broke a window, the juvenile would work to earn the money to replace the window. There is no restitution if the parents pay for the window at no cost to the juvenile. The juvenile has to take personal responsibility and pay for the window. It also includes doing community service to restore the community to its previous state before the juvenile damaged the community.

A probation officer would oversee the process to make sure the parents and the juvenile acted in a responsible manner. At the end of the process, a successful probation evaluation would state that the problems were solved.

Suicide Evaluation and Counseling

Juveniles sometime threaten to kill themselves. They might not mean it and even may be exaggerating. However, over time juveniles may actually kill themselves. No chances are ever taken, even if the juvenile does not seem serious. This threat could also be a cry for help. It has happened enough so that all private and public agencies take any statement of suicide very seriously and rush the juvenile to suicide evaluation by a professional and provide services where needed.

Mental Health

Mentally ill and mentally impaired services are specialized and very expensive. These services are normally long term, depending on the diagnosis and level of impairment. As you go from neurosis to psychosis, the ability to deal with everyday life goes down. Neurosis is where there is a mental health problem but the juvenile is able to function in society. A typical neurosis would be an abnormal fear of heights. Psychosis is more serious and the juvenile is usually not able to function in normal society. An example of a serious psychosis is fear of leaving home so that the juvenile cannot go to the store or attend public school. Impaired individuals have less and less coping skills to deal with everyday life. These specialized services are provided after extensive interviews and testing of mental and emotional abilities and stabilities.

Sex Offenders

Sex offender programs are specialized counseling services for juveniles and adults, often mandated by the courts and state laws. To the best knowledge of the authors, there are few tested results for these intervention programs. The bulk of the research indicates that many sex offenders repeat their crimes. There is a need for better services.

The Violent Offender

Violent offenders are usually held in secure facilities, they are mostly males from inner cities, poor minority neighborhoods dominated by single mother families and unemployed adult males. A great deal of inner city juvenile violence comes from drug and gang related activities.

Reality therapy where the juvenile is taught to deal with his future and present in a realistic manner has seen some success. Psychotherapy and psychological one-on-one counseling has had a limited success. Violent juveniles are involved with group therapy in

47

many programs. These group therapies are usually not evaluated for success or failure.

A major issue for the juvenile authorities is how to deal with the violent juveniles, future since sending them back to gang-dominated neighborhoods is a bad choice. Many of these juveniles spend their adolescent years in a series of secure institutions; group homes and foster care located a good distance from their old neighborhoods and their biological families. The overall failure rate with violent juveniles, nationally, has been extremely high. This failure rate, over the years, has been documented by a history of arrests and juvenile and adult court appearances by these violent juveniles. These are the most expensive juveniles in the system and their lifetime care and prosecution by government authorities runs into the hundreds of thousand of dollars for each case.

Vocational Training and Alternate Schools

Vocational training refers to programs that provide education and training for jobs that youths can qualify for with a high school diploma. Many of these programs take place in public and private schools that are **alternate schools** to the normal public school curriculum. All of these schools normally lead to a high school diploma. These programs provide training in small engine repair, cosmetology, computers, carpentry and plumbing and mechanics for cars and trucks to list a few examples. They also normally have smaller classes and a great deal of individual help.

Tutors

Students who cannot attend public schools for reasons of sickness or disruptive behavior still have to be provided an education by public law. The public school system has to provide tutors and pay for these tutors. The tutors go to the student's home and each student has to pass exams in order to graduate with a high school diploma.

Court Services

Juvenile judges routinely advise juveniles of their rights. See the chapter on United States Supreme Court decisions for an explanation of these rights. Courts also order public and private agencies to provide services to juveniles. Some of these services include housing, counseling with emphasis on drug and alcohol counseling. Parents and guardians have been known to physically abuse their children. Judges can remove juveniles from abusive homes and offer protection of the courts to the juveniles. In the most extreme situations judges can permanently remove all parental rights in cases of severe and continuing abuse of the juveniles.

Juvenile Detention

Juveniles, when they are taken from their home, are placed in a temporary facility where they stay until a court decides what to do with them. Temporary can mean anything from a few days to a few months but it is never a permanent placement. The juveniles, by court order, could be released to their parents or guardians or sent to a public or private facility until they are adults. The court could also send the juveniles to facilities such as foster care, a group home or a secure or non-secure institution. Detention facilities wish to provide safe custody in a restricted environment for their juvenile clients and generally provide limited counseling services. To help the court in deciding what to do with the juvenile, detention facilities provide observation and assessments/evaluations of the juvenile. Psychometric tests, which are standardized psychological tests, are used when needed. They also allow visitation by parents and guardians.

Community-Based Juvenile Services

If the family is supportive and the youth lives in a safe neighborhood, it is better to provide services in the community. **Family counseling** looks at the relationship of all members of a household living in the same house. Many juvenile lower class families have many problems that need to be dealt with if the juvenile is to have a successful life. These could be public health problems, drug and alcohol abuse and the need for financial counseling. Adults may need anger and violence control counseling. A great deal of professional intervention may be needed if a juvenile is to have a chance to make it. There may be a needed referral to psychological and human services counselors as well.

Youth Court

This is an informal court run by high school students and supported by the local bar association, the public schools and local government youth services. Youths act as judges, defenders, prosecutors, and probation officers and render judgments with punishments mostly consisting of community services. It is highly supported by most communities. When fights, or class disruptions happen on school grounds, for example, this court makes a judgment. The youth judges are tough on the students and do not let them get away with anything. If the issues cannot be solved in youth court, then the issues go on to the juvenile courts.

Parenting Classes and Tough Love

Parenting skills are not automatic and need to be learned. Parents with aggressive and troublesome children and adolescents especially need a support group and need to learn successful parenting skills like how to set boundaries and enforce these boundaries.

Parents need to express their love to their children so that the children recognize that their parents do care for them. Juveniles also understand fair play. Warm loving parents with boundaries for behavior consistently enforced is the most successful parenting model. Tough Love is a movement for dealing with aggressive children and youth. It works best when it is a support program for parents.

Tough love may become a brutalizing program for teens that are institutionalized. (www.washingtonpost.com/wpdyn/content/article/2006/01/28/AR2006012800062_pf.html) is very critical of tough love); (http://www.4troubledteens.com/toughlove.html) is supportive of the tough love approach for parents.

Transfers

The juvenile can be transferred, with few restrictions, throughout the state system to both public and private facilities. In some cases the transfer may take a court order unless the law gives the state agency the authority to transfer the juvenile. Where the juvenile is transferred to depends mainly on the availability of a bed for the juvenile. Other transfer criteria are the need for security based on the dangerousness of the juvenile and special counseling and medical needs. Examples of special needs would be drug and alcohol abuse, and crimes of rape and arson.

Moving On Into The System

The juvenile can go from community placement in foster care to secure institutions. In most cases the juvenile will go back to the parents or guardians with services. The goal of the juvenile justice system is to offer services to help the juvenile and the family becomes successful citizens. If the juvenile is violent and engages in fights or initially is engaged in armed robberies, he or she is likely to become more involved in the secure system in order to protect the community from this violence, Otherwise, the system would prefer to place him or her with the parents or guardians in the community.

Leaving the Juvenile Justice System

This takes a court order and a safe home to go to. The court has to be assured that the juvenile will have a home with adequate guardians or parents along with food, clothing and shelter. Depending on the offenses the juvenile has committed, this may be very simple or very complicated. Skipping school simply means that the parents or guardians need to enforce school attendance. A juvenile rapist, arsonist or murderer is obviously a more difficult case.

Conclusion

This chapter was written to make the readers know about the services that are available for juveniles in trouble and what happens to juveniles in the juvenile justice system. Law dictates much about what happens to juveniles but juveniles, parents and guardians have many choices to help these youths out. Knowing about these services can make a huge difference in a troubled youth's life and future life choices. Juvenile judges have great pf discretion in providing services and placing juveniles in various agencies and institutions. Probation may recommend placement and services but it is up to the juvenile judge as to what will happen to the juvenile.

CHAPTER

4

Juvenile Court Procedures

Chapter Outline

Comparison of Juvenile Court to Adult Criminal Court

As the juveniles become involved in the Juvenile Court Process there is a need to understand the similarities and differences between the Juvenile Courts and Adult Criminal Courts. The major difference is language but there are also some legal issues.

53

Comparison Chart for Juvenile and Adult Criminal Courts

Juvenile Legal Proceedings	Adult Criminal Legal Proceedings
1. Taken into custody or arrested	1. Arrested by police officer
2. Petition sent to juvenile judge. Can be initiated by police, parents, schools, social service agencies and any citizen. Prepared by a local probation agency	2. District attorney indictment in criminal court through filed information with the court for misdemeanor or a grand jury for a felony
3. Initial appearance: admits or denies facts or amended facts	3. Arraignment: adult pleads guilty or not guilty.
4. Fact Finding Bench Trial (Judge Trial)	4. Criminal trial with a jury, or a plea bargain with a guilty plea.
5. Adjudication where case is guilty or not guilty of the crime. adjudicated a delinquent or person in need of supervision.	5. Jury or judge finds adults dismissed or juvenile A guilty judgment is an adult conviction.
6. Disposition Hearing	6. Sentencing Hearing

Petition Process

Juveniles are referred to the court through a petition process, usually initiated through a local probation department. Police take juveniles into custody. Juveniles are apprehended in most jurisdictions, while adults are arrested. Police may also give juveniles appearance tickets in many jurisdictions. An appearance ticket commands the juvenile to appear in juvenile court. The juvenile behavior may be related to a delinquency act such as an adult crime like burglary. The act could be a pure juvenile offense labeled a status offense resulting in a finding of a person in need of supervision. Examples of a status offense are skipping school, home runaways, drinking alcoholic beverages or defying parental authority.

Parents likewise may initiate a complaint petition, which is common practice. School authorities may initiate a complaint petition to juvenile court for such conduct as truancy (not going to school), disruptive behavior, along with drug and alcohol abuse.

Welfare and social services agencies refer juveniles to the Courts for risky or criminal behavior. This may be the result of an investigation of a family after a complaint. For example, a juvenile running away from a group home or foster care may result in a court referral. Probation refers juveniles to the court as part of the normal petition process and when juveniles on probation violate the rules.

Fact Finding Hearing

The Juvenile Court hearings are never jury trials since the United States Supreme Court has ruled that juveniles have no constitutional right to a jury trial. Instead, a juvenile is provided a hearing before a single judge. This is sometimes called a bench trial. The judge can then assess and weigh the merits of the case as to further processing or dismiss the case. In the case of dismissal the judge would release the juvenile to the juvenile's guardians, parents or government agency. The judge may dismiss the case at any time and may refer the case to probation at any time. The **adjudication** would be a finding of fact that the juvenile is delinquent or is a person in need of supervision. Cases are most often dismissed because there is lack of evidence or there are major problems with the evidence. Juveniles are never convicted of an actual crime in juvenile court. Juveniles are found to be delinquent or a person in need of supervision.

The Juvenile Defense Lawyer
Also Known As The Law Guardian

Juveniles, parents and guardians can hire a lawyer or have a court appointed lawyer, also called a legal guardian in some jurisdictions.

This juvenile defense lawyer legally represents the juvenile and is concerned that the juvenile be treated fairly.

Juveniles have three ways to have a lawyer represent them:

1. Private lawyers
2. Public defender or law guardian provided by the court
3. Court appointed lawyers are called assigned counsel. They are appointed from a list of lawyers provided by the local bar association.

The parents can hire a lawyer to represent the juvenile, with one exception. If the parents were involved in the court petition, then the parent's lawyer would have a conflict of interest. For example, if the parents are seeking a PINS petition against the juvenile, the lawyer cannot represent both the parents and the juvenile. The juvenile may not want to accept a PINS petition. In this case, the juvenile needs a separate lawyer to represent the juvenile. Some judges may be stricter and feel that any time a parent pays a lawyer's fee, the lawyer could only represent the parent's interest.

A lawyer of their own choosing should represent minors in Juvenile Court. This is also true for Appeals Court where the appeal is coming from Juvenile Court. A law guardian who is a lawyer representing minors in Juvenile Court may be appointed by a Judge. A minor is presumed by the court to lack the needed knowledge and maturity to represent herself or himself. This is one reason why the court appoints a lawyer or law guardian to represent the minor. The Supreme Court in "In Re Gault" made legal representation a constitutional right for minors in Juvenile Court.

The juvenile will have the help of a lawyer when going to juvenile court. Normally, a lawyer from the district attorney's office will bring the case against the juvenile. In some jurisdictions, a lawyer from the County Attorney's Office or Corporation Council may be designated by the district attorney to prosecute juvenile cases. The judge presides in juvenile court and decides on detention and if it will be secure or non-secure. The juvenile court judge reviews evidence and decides if it is adequate. The judge also decides if the case should be heard in juvenile or adult criminal court.

The initial appearance of a juvenile is much the same as the arraignment for adults. This Juvenile Proceeding is called a Fact Finding Hearing. Adults plead guilty or not guilty. The juvenile Admits to the Petition Facts or Enters a Denial Plea.

To admit to the Petition Facts is to plead guilty and to deny the Petition Facts is to plead not guilty. This language is so different from normal adult criminal courts that it is somewhat misleading and confusing for most citizens. The language needs to be carefully explained to parents, guardians and most of all to the youths and juveniles who are the subject of all these procedures.

Juvenile Court Transfers and Adult Criminal Court Jurisdiction

However, before this plea process can proceed, the judge has to state if juvenile court has proper jurisdiction depending on the age of the juvenile and the severity of the crime. This jurisdiction decision determines the authority of hearing the case, that is, which is in charge, juvenile or adult criminal court. Having jurisdiction means the juvenile court can legally hear the juvenile's case.

States have many different laws concerning juvenile and adult criminal court jurisdiction. Jurisdiction concerns whether the adult criminal court or the juvenile court will try the case. One item is age. In New York State, the act has to take place before age sixteen to be a juvenile case. In California the act has to be before age of eighteen. Most states have eighteen as the age when adult criminal courts would have jurisdiction.

Jurisdiction also depends on the criminal act. In many states certain serious crimes such as murder, armed robbery, aggravated assault and rape may be tried in adult criminal court depending on the juvenile's age at the time of the crime. In other states serious felonies are transferred to adult criminal court from juvenile court. In other states juvenile and adult criminal court have joint jurisdiction. A judge makes a decision as to whether adult or juvenile court has jurisdiction for each case. In most states, the judge and the district attorney have to agree to the transfer to adult criminal court from juvenile court. Most district attorneys would rather have most juvenile cases heard in juvenile court.

Juveniles go from juvenile court to adult court in three ways depending upon state law (Siegel, Welsh and Senna, 2006):

1. **Judicial Waiver,** where the judicial court gives up its jurisdiction over the juvenile and the adult criminal court then has jurisdiction, thereby the trial takes place in adult criminal court.
2. **Adult criminal court has original jurisdiction** by state law because of the serious felony the juvenile has committed with age of the juvenile being a factor.
3. Both adult criminal court and juvenile court have **concurrent jurisdiction** which means the juvenile can be prosecuted in either court.

Basically adult criminal courts, jails and prisons do not want to have anything to do with juveniles and are quite relieved when juvenile court keeps jurisdiction over the juvenile. The US Supreme has ruled that the district attorney only gets one chance to prosecute the juvenile, be it juvenile court or adult criminal court. It is unconstitutional to be tried twice for the same crime. This is the principle of double jeopardy. In the past when district attorneys lost a case in adult court, they transferred the case to juvenile court to try the juvenile a second time. Transfers to adult court in order to get tough on crime have been a troublesome issue and at least one state simply abolished its juvenile courts. (Breed Versus Jones, 1975 (421U.S.519, 95S.Ct., 1770 (1975: Trying juveniles in juvenile court and then again in adult court is double jeopardy and is therefore unconstitutional.)

We have many different laws concerning juvenile jurisdiction in all fifty states. The complications are because of the variability of each state's laws pertaining to the way juvenile constitutional rights are processed. However, the juvenile court judge will sort this out and tell everyone in a ruling at the initial appearance. The law guardian can be a big help. If the case does go to adult criminal court, the juvenile will have more constitutional rights but the punishments may be harsher.

Mental Capacity

A question that comes up at these hearings is whether or not the juvenile understands what is going on. If there are reasons to suspect some kind of mental problem or other disability, the judge will adjourn the court process and order psychological/medical evaluation such as a hearing on mental capacity. This can be fairly extensive.

Pleading Guilty and Innocent: Accepting and Denying The Facts

The juvenile, with the advice of his or her appointed lawyer, also called a law guardian, pleads guilty or innocent in front of a juvenile court judge. However, the language is different from adult criminal court and there is no right to a jury trial (Schall V Martin, 1984). *When a juvenile admits to the facts, the juvenile admits to doing the crime or non-criminal status offense.* This is how the juvenile pleads guilty in juvenile court.

When a juvenile admits to amended facts, this means that the original charges are changed and the judge agrees to the change. For example, a burglary may be amended to trespassing. The juvenile then agrees to the amended fact, which is a plea of guilty in juvenile court. Plea to an amended fact has been compared to plea-bargaining in adult criminal court. The judge adjudicates the juvenile as a juvenile delinquent for committing an act that would be a crime if the juvenile were an adult. The judge adjudicates a person in need of supervision for committing non-criminal status offenses.

To plead not guilty, the juvenile denies the facts. If this takes place at the initial hearing, the judge schedules a fact-finding hearing. The juvenile judge at the end of fact finding, where witnesses and evidence is heard, rules whether the juvenile did the crime or status offense or not. If the judge rules that the juvenile did not do the crime or status offense, the juvenile is then remanded into the hands of parents or guardians. This is the same as a not guilty ruling in adult criminal court. If the judge rules that the juvenile did the crime or status offense, the proceeding goes to the disposition stage. To do this, the judge would adjudicate the juvenile as a delinquent or person in need of supervision.

Predisposition Reports

The disposition stage is compared to the sentencing in adult criminal court. Before the disposition, the judge needs to have some information on the juvenile in order to do what is best for the child. The probation department prepares this report for the judge. It includes the same social history prepared on a juvenile at the petition stage but is more detailed and extensive, including interviews and contact with family, friends, social service agencies, the police and the schools. It may also include psychological and attitude testing such as the MMPI for mental state, values and attitudes, aggressiveness and social skills.

The following was covered in chapter 1 and contains the major elements of the predisposition report:

Elements of the Social History
Information needed for predispositions report and referral into the juvenile justice system
- Description
- The Offense
- History of the Youth's Behavior
- The Family
- Personal Traits and Strengths
- Peers and Friendships
- School
- Drugs and Alcohol Abuse
- Medical History Including Emotional and Physical Disability
- Conclusion

The Assessment Model
- Risk Assessment
- Need Assessment
- Strength Assessment
- Assessment and Diversion

At the end of the report, the probation officer will make a disposition recommendation (sentencing for an adult) based on a needs assessment and the risk of the juvenile harming other citizens and the community.

What happens to the juvenile may affect the juvenile for a lifetime. Bad behavior can be stopped here while the adolescent builds a life for the future or it can lead to a life of crime, drug and alcohol abuse and failure. How these decisions are made and the information used for these decisions is important to officials in the system, juveniles, parents and guardians. These are what are called **life decisions**, decisions that you live with all your life: dropping out of school, going to college and choosing a major, having a baby, marriage and divorce. The results of a disposition (sentencing) may last a lifetime. The records are normally sealed but police and military background checks may open them up.

This report is similar to the presentence report and is prepared for the court mostly by the local probation agency and sometimes by social services for disposition (sentencing) of the juveniles. In larger jurisdictions a committee of professionals from probation, social services, and mental health may prepare it.

Minimum Standards For A Predisposition/Presentencing Report

1. Legal History of the offender includes:
   - Previous convictions and
   - Institutional record,
   - Description of the present offense,
   - Statement of the person charging the complaint,
   - Statement of the juvenile offender concerning the offense,
   - Mitigating or aggravating circumstances of the present offense,
   - Others involved in the present offense,
   - Description of attitudes and behavior during detention.
2. The juvenile offender's social history includes development, education, physical and mental health, leisure time activities and vocational interests.
3. Social agency and mental health agency contact only if the juvenile has been a client of any public or private agencies. This includes any services or outcomes provided. Social evaluations may include psychological evaluations, risk, needs, and strength assessments.
4. The probation officer or professionals from another reporting social service agency writes a summary and recommendation. The summary and recommendation is the most important part of the report. The juvenile defense lawyer should pay special attention to this report and recommendation and correct any facts that may

---

not be true. The juvenile defense lawyer should sit down at a scheduled private meeting with the juvenile and the parents or guardians to discuss this report and the consequences of the recommendation.

Once the judge receives the completed predisposition/presentence report and its recommendations, the judgment of the court is entered.

Sentencing, Disposition and Placement

In juvenile court, judges may exercise options in the sentencing/disposition process. The court may admonish a stern warning to juveniles and remand them to their parents or guardians. It may place the juvenile on probation with fines, restitution or community service and have the juvenile report to a probation officer over a period of time. The court may take a more restrictive disposition and take the juvenile out of his or her home and place the juvenile in foster care, group homes, camps/ranches or secure institution. Most placements are in state and only go out of state if there are no openings in the juvenile's home state. Juvenile with special needs have a wide variety of placements.

Special Needs Placements

1. Emotionally disturbed juveniles who need psychological services.
2. Severely restricted secure placements because of violent behavior.
3. A victim of physical and/or emotional abuse with a need for special counseling services.
4. A retarded juvenile who needs special services and a special needs supportive environment.
5. Juveniles who have major alcohol and drug abuse problems.

Community based placements, such as returning the juvenile to the home and probation, are felt by many professionals to reduce the negative stigmas that being involved with the justice system entails, like being arrested and jailed. A juvenile remaining with their family, rather than being shipped to an institution, requires fewer adjustments and disruptions in the juvenile's life. Over all, over the years of analysis, community placements seem to cost fewer taxpayer dollars.

Conclusion

Fact Finding Hearings can take place within a few hours of the initial hearing or many weeks later. The juvenile appears with his or her juvenile defense lawyer, and parents or guardians. In some courts the language would be to admit to the charges, admit to a lesser charge or deny the charge. The juvenile gets a chance to tell the judge his or her side of the story. If it looks like the juvenile is innocent or doesn't need any services, then the case is dismissed. If the juvenile is adjudicated (convicted) the juvenile defense lawyer and assigned probation officer must pay special attention to the summary and recommendation of the predisposition and inform the juvenile, parents or guardians of the meaning of this report and recommendation.

Most juvenile courts try to lessen the justice system's impact on the juveniles' and family life unless there is violence, gang activity and/or a long history of lawlessness. The community, local government and most juveniles and parents would prefer that juvenile problems be solved within the family. It is only when juvenile problems spill out of the family that that most courts are willing to intervene. Again, this means very serious activity, like an arrest or a serious intervention by the police, social workers or the schools before juvenile incidents are brought to the attention of the juvenile courts. Juvenile justice is an extremely reluctant system of intervention.

CHAPTER

5

Major Court Cases In Juvenile Justice

Chapter Outline

Introduction

The Juvenile Justice Court throughout the United States is a civil court that tries both civil and what should be criminal juvenile cases. Some of these cases involve adult crimes. The also involve offenses that would not be criminal if the youth was an adult, such as running away from home. Juvenile delinquency is not a crime even if a 13-year-old youth tortured and murdered a helpless 70-year-old grandmother. Juvenile court and family court are legally civil courts. Civil courts do not legally try criminal cases. So the above juvenile would be adjudicated a juvenile delinquent rather than convicted of a horrible crime.

Juveniles need the same protection by the law and the constitution that adults have. Because of the tender ages of most youths, they should have more protection than adults. The reality is that juveniles have less constitutional protection than adults in the United States. For example, juveniles have no right of bail, today, according to the U.S. Supreme Court. Juveniles, however, do have more than an extra right that adults do not have. Juveniles cannot be executed. Juveniles have gained very substantial constitutional rights beginning in 1966 and 1967 and this is their story.

Ex Parte Crouse—Philadelphia, 1839

Sixty years before the first statewide juvenile court in Cook County, Illinois, was created in 1899, a Pennsylvania juvenile justice case in 1839 took away the due process proceedings of the Bill of Rights from juveniles. It was the case of Mary Ann Crouse who had been given into the jurisdiction of the Philadelphia House of Refuge by her mother.

The case was named after the last name of the child, " **Ex Parte Crouse**". The Supreme Court of Pennsylvania, is cited as, 4 Whart. 9 (1839). The case has been misidentified in hundreds of textbooks as an 1838 case but its real date is 1839 (Parry, 2005, 45). This case never rose to the level of the U.S. Supreme Court, yet its precedent and reasoning prevailed throughout the centuries and the country.

The child's mother, Mary Crouse, delivered Mary Ann Crouse to the Philadelphia House of Refuge. Her father wanted her back but the Court refused to release her based on a doctrine of **parens patrae,** where the courts and the country became the parent of the child. This means that the parent's legal rights over their children ceased to exist by court order. Let us examine the judge's words as he wrote his infamous decision denying all parental rights and all Due Process to American youths and children for over 137 years. (The quotes are from **Ex Parte Crouse**, Parry, 2005:45–46.)

"The petition for habeas corpus was in the name of the father. . . ." This court in 1839 and the juvenile laws over these many years, use the word infant to designate the juveniles and adolescents under their jurisdiction. The Juvenile Court uses the reason of "infancy" to deny juveniles due process adult rights. The juvenile who needs to be protected by the court, should have more rights than adults.

A Philadelphia Magistrate said he had proof of vicious conduct by Mary Ann Crouse, but with no specifics. The court also used the word "incorrigible" which is a word with no content, used to justify commitment to juvenile prisons from the 19th through the 21st century.

The judge then gave these infamous words to the ages (Parry, 2005:45-46)

"The House of Refuge is not a prison but a school. Where reformation and not punishment is an end, it may indeed be used as a prison for juvenile convicts who else would be committed to a common gaol {jail}. . . . The object of charity is reformation by training its inmates to industry, by imbuing the minds with the principles of morality and religion, by furnishing them with a means to earn a living and above all by separating them from the influence of corrupt associates. To this end may not the natural parents when unequal to the task or education or unworthy of it may not the proper parent be superseded by parens patrae or common guardians of the community. . . . As to abridgement of indefensible rights by confinement of the person, it is no more than that which is borne in every school."

These schools became known as reformatory schools. From 1838 to the 21st century most reform schools operated as prisons where juveniles were often treated more cruelly than adults. The legal fiction of labeling them schools hides the cruel reality from the public. More recently the juvenile justice system used such meaningless word as camps or *centers* as in juvenile centers. Industrial school was a favorite to show that the juveniles were industrious. The school label continues to this day. Even when juveniles and "infants" have been treated humanely in confinement, these juvenile prisons have never been simply public schools.

Most, but not all, of these juvenile confinements have been forced over the years to reform. Most juvenile institutions today, are inspected and treat juveniles in a more humane manner. It is always worth a visit to any juvenile institution to observe the realities of the confinements of the youth. Always read the bulletin boards to get an idea of the day-to-day activities of the confined, institutional life of the juveniles. Find out from interviewing the residents what type of punishments is used by the staff. Anyone who has a juvenile that is incarcerated, has an ethical duty to inspect these facilities.

Ex Parte Crouse   Philadelphia, 1839 established for 137 years that:

- Parens patriae and locus parentis apply to all juvenile cases and the state has the legal right to replace the biological parents and cut off all parental legal rights to their children.
- Due process does not apply to juvenile proceedings.
- Juvenile civil proceedings are not criminal proceedings and do not provide juveniles with the constitutional due process rights that adults enjoy.
- Juvenile secure institutions are not prisons but instead are to be considered as schools whose purpose is to reform wayward and troubled juveniles.

The **Ex Parte Crouse** decision created a great deal of contradictions, which became part of the juvenile justice system throughout U.S. history.

Introduction to Kent v. United States and In Re Gault

The first case that made any significant changes, and they were narrow changes, for the federal courts was in 1966. *Kent v. United States* happened in the District of Columbia and is a federal case that only applies to federal proceedings and does not apply to the states. The second case in 1967, *In Re Gault,* applied to all the states and provided basic due process right for juveniles. Subsequent cases have added to these two due process cases in significant ways over the years.

These major changes in juvenile justice took place because of the stories of two very different youths: *Morris Kent, a juvenile criminal in Washington, D.C and Gerald Gault a rather innocent juvenile and ordinary American boy living in Giles County, Arizona.* The full story of these two boys will help all of us understand how the courts work with two very real and nationally important cases.

Kent v. United States—Washington, D.C., 1966

Morris Kent came to the attention of the juvenile court when at the age of 14; he was involved in several house breakings and an attempted purse snatching. He was placed on probation, while living with his single mother and had a "social service" file. On September 2, 1961 when Morris was 16, he entered the apartment of a woman in the District of Columbia, took her wallet and raped her. Morris was caught through his fingerprints, which were on file from his probation sentence and picked up at 3 P.M. on September 5, 1961. For seven hours the police, without having a lawyer or parent present, interrogated him. He admitted to the crime and other house breakings, robberies and rapes. He slept over at the receiving home for children and was interrogated again at police headquarters the next day. His mother was never notified of his arrest but at 2:00 P.M. on September 6, Morris' mother arrived with a lawyer and talked with social services.

Morris' mother found out that juvenile court wanted to give up their jurisdiction (waived) and have Morris tried in Adult Criminal Court for his adult crimes. She opposed this and her lawyer had Morris interviewed by two psychiatrists and one psychologist with the resulting opinion that Morris suffered severe psychopathology and should be treated at a psychiatric hospital. The defense lawyer wanted Morris tried in juvenile court and the lawyer asked to see Morris' social service file so he could provide an adequate defense.

The juvenile judge who had access to the social service file, never met with the defense lawyer or Morris' mother and ignored their requests. This judge said that "after full investigation" that Morris would be tried in adult criminal court. The social service file did state that Morris had a mental illness. The defense counsel was never allowed by the judge to see Morris' social service file. Morris was tried in the Federal District Court, which was the adult criminal court. The defense counsel said that the waiver to adult criminal court was illegal. A jury convicted Morris of six counts of house breaking and robbery and he was sentenced to 30 to 90 years in prison. He would get out of prison at a minimum of age 46 and a maximum of age 106. The defense lawyer appealed and the case ended up in the U.S. Supreme Court.

Justice Abe Fortes wrote the majority opinion. He agreed with the 1839 Mary Ann Crouse case that the state could replace the parents but disagreed strongly about what that meant in treating juveniles fairly and constitutionally, "The State is parens patrae rather than prosecuting attorney and judge. But the admonition to function in a 'parental' relationships is not an invitation to procedural arbitrariness." Remember that the judge simply ignored the concerns and requests of the defense lawyer.

Supreme Court Justice Fortas felt that the government has a special mandate to protect children. He went on to say "that he {meaning the juvenile} receives the worst of both worlds: that he gets neither the protection accorded to adults nor the solicitous care and regenerative treatment postulated for children." He meant in plain English that juveniles are denied the due process rights of adults and never had the support and kindness of parental care of the court acting as parent. The juvenile had neither good care nor adult's rights. So, the court decided to give juveniles some due process adult rights after the judge wrote the following,

"there is no place in our system of law for reaching a result of such tremendous consequence without ceremony—without hearing—without effective assistance of counsel, without a statement of reasons. It is inconceivable that a court of justice dealing with adults with respect to a similar issue, would proceed in this manner"

Kent v. United States, 1966, the US Supreme Court decided that in federal court cases where juvenile court waives its jurisdiction and transfers the juvenile to adult criminal court, the juvenile is entitled to:

1. A full hearing on the issue of transfer to the adult criminal court.
2. The assistance of legal counsel at the hearing.
3. Full access to the social records used to determine whether such transfers should be made.
4. A statement of the reasons why the juvenile judge decided to waive the juvenile to adult criminal court.

Chapter 5

In Re Gault—Arizona, 1967

Gerald Gault was a normal American boy with no criminal record. A Mrs. Cook accused Gerald of making lewd or indecent remarks to her in a telephone call. The court described these remarks as "the irritating, offensive, sex variety. This was a verbal complaint and there was no other record. No record of what Gerald may have actually said was stated in the US Supreme Court decision and Mrs. Cook was never asked to testify.

On this weak evidence, Gerald and a friend, Ronald Lewis, were taken into custody by the Sheriff of Gila County around 10:00 A. M. on June 8, 1964 and brought to the detention center. Gerald was under a probation order for being in the company of another boy who had stolen a woman's wallet. Gerald's mother and father were at work and were never notified of Gerald's arrest. They found out what happened to Gerald from the Lewis family and went to visit him at the detention center.

The next day there was a hearing on June 9 at 3:00 P.M. and the probation officer and superintendent of the detention center, Officer Flagg filed a petition concerning Gerald, with the court. Gerald's parents did not get to see the petition until they filed a habeas corpus hearing on August 17. Officer Flagg's petition recited no facts but simply said, "said minor is under the age of eighteen and is in need of protection of this Honorable Court; said minor is a delinquent minor." The petition asked for a hearing and decision regarding "the care and custody of said minor." At June 9th hearing, Gerald and his mother and brother showed up with officer Flagg for a hearing in the judge's chambers. No record of the hearing was made. Mrs. Cook never appeared at this hearing or any other proceeding. Only officer Flagg talked to her on the phone on June 9, 1964.

There was the usual adolescent mix-up concerning the Mrs. Cook phone call as people tried to remember what was said at this unrecorded hearing. What we know came out from what people said at the August 16 habeas corpus hearing. Gerald's mother recalled that Gerald said he only dialed the phone and handed it to his friend Ronald. Officer Flagg said that Gerald admitting to making one of the lewd statements. Judge McGhee said that Gerald admitted to making one of these statements. At the end of the June 9th hearing, Judge McGhee said he would "think about it" and Gerald was taken back to the detention center. On June 11 or 12, Gerald was released and driven home.

Officer Flagg sent a signed note to Gerald's mother, handwritten on a plain piece of paper which said, *"Judge McGHEE has set Monday, June 15, 1964 at 11:00 A.M. as the date and time for further Hearings on Gerald's delinquency."*

The contradictory testimony continued at the unrecorded June 15 hearing. We only know what went on when the conflicted memories poured forth at the August15 habeas corpus hearing. Gerald, Gerald's mother and father, Ronald Lewis and his father, officer Flagg and Henderson showed up before Judge McGhee. Mr. and Mrs. Gault remembered that Gerald testified that he only dialed the number and the other boy had made the remarks.

Officer Flagg remembered that Gerald did not admit to the lewd remarks at the June 15 hearing. Judge McGhee remembered, "there was some admission of some of the lewd statements. He didn't admit any of the more serious lewd statements." Mrs. Gault asked that Mrs. Cook be present "so she see which boy had done the talking, had done the dirty talking over the phone." A referral report by the probation officer was filed with the court charging Gerald with "Lewd Phone Calls". At the end of the hearing Judge McGhee committed Gerald to the state industrial school until the age of 21, "until sooner discharged by process of law." Gerald was found guilty and sentenced to six years imprisonment for Lewd Phone Calls.

If Gerald was an adult, he would have been sentenced under Arizona Law 13-377 which made it a misdemeanor if, in the presence or hearing of any woman or child a person uses vulgar, abusive or obscene language. The penalty was a fine of $5 to $50 and jail up to two months. The law did not apply to males who heard vulgar, etc. language. As a juvenile delinquent, who was also denied due process, Gerald was snatched from the streets of Arizona, jailed in a detention facility and then sentenced to six years imprisonment in an industrial school. When you cannot leave an institution without being arrested, it is obviously a jail.

The cases go on with the Judge's faulty memory about other minor acts, like the judge hearing that Gerald might have stolen a baseball glove. There was no hearing because the judge said the case lacked a "material foundation". That means there was no evidence. The judge said that Gerald had admitted to making other silly or funny calls. The Superior Court of Arizona dismissed the habeas corpus. The Supreme Court of Arizona got the case on appeal and dismissed Gerald's conviction as unconstitutional because of numerous violations of Gerald's rights under due process of law, such as hearsay testimony.

The U.S. Supreme Court agreed with this judgment. **In Re Gault** *in* **1967** *established the following due process rights for juveniles in juvenile proceedings in state courts.*

1. Notice of charges including parent and legal guardians being notified.
2. Right to counsel, that means having a defense lawyer to represent the juvenile.
3. Right to confrontation of accusers and cross-examination of anyone who accuses a juvenile of an offense or crime.
4. The privilege against self-incrimination means the juvenile can refuse to testify against himself or herself. For adults, this is the fifth amendment of the US constitution.
5. Right to a transcript, that is a written record, of all court proceedings.
6. Right to appellate review. This means if a lower court decides the juvenile is guilty, the juvenile can ask a higher court to look over the case and agree with the guilty verdict or overturn the guilty verdict.

In Re Winship—New York State, 1970

Winship, a 12-year-old boy stole $112.00 from a woman's pocket-book in New York State. An adult would normally serve less than a year in jail for this type of larceny. Winship was sentenced to a training school for 18 months, which could be extended up to six years. The highest court in NYS, the Court of Appeals made this decision since NYS law 744 only demanded the lower limit of civil proof, which is a preponderance of evidence. NYS argued that this was the standard of proof for civil courts and the state's juvenile court (Family court) is a civil court. The US Supreme Court agreed that the juvenile court was a civil court. However, the court said that the higher standard of proof used by criminal court was needed when juveniles were accused of committing a crime to ensure a greater degree of safety for the juvenile given the juvenile's presumption of innocence. The US Supreme Court felt this was necessary for the juvenile to have a fair due process hearing. **Due Process for juveniles includes the stricter rule of proof beyond a reasonable doubt of adult criminal court rather than the preponderance of evidence of a civil court standard.**

McKeiver v. Pennsylvania—1971

Juvenile proceedings are not the same as adult criminal court proceedings. In an earlier case, Duncan v. Louisiana, the US Supreme Court agreed that the sixth amendment of the US Constitution guaranteed a jury trial to an adult who committed serious crimes. The McKeiver case turned the previous decision 180 degrees around and denied this right to juveniles. Joseph McKeiver, age 16, was accused of three felonies under Pennsylvania law, robbery, larceny and receiving stolen goods. He was adjudicated a delinquent by a juvenile court judge and placed on probation after he asked for a jury trial. The US Supreme Court decided this case and two other juvenile cases who had also asked for a jury trial, The Court said that In Re Gault did not include a jury trial in its due process decision and a jury trial was not necessary for fact finding. The court did not want to change a juvenile arbitration process into an adversary process. A jury trial could result in delay, formality and the possibility of a public trial and a public trial was not provided for in most jurisdictions. States deny a jury trial to juveniles because the U.S. Supreme Court let them. Justice Blackmun did say if a state wanted to institute a jury trial for juveniles the state could do this. This has never happened. **Juveniles do not have a constitutional right to a trial by jury.**

Breed v. Jones—1975

The juvenile is being tried twice for the same crime. Jones, age 17, was adjudicated a delinquent in California courts based on a finding, after a hearing with testimony, that Jones had committed a robbery. The court found Jones, at a dispositional hearing (sentencing), unfit for treatment in juvenile court and his case was transferred to adult criminal court. He was tried, found guilty of robbery and sentenced to the California Youth Authority. He objected and said this was double jeopardy. Double jeopardy is: you cannot be tried for the same crime twice. Once a decision has been made in juvenile court, a juvenile cannot be tried again in adult criminal court. **Trying juveniles in juvenile court and then again in adult court is double jeopardy and is therefore unconstitutional.**

Oklahoma Publishing Co. v. District Court—1977

An 11-year-old boy's photograph was taken at a detention hearing where the boy was accused of homicide. The photograph was published in the newspaper and the D.A. tried to stop any further publication. The US Supreme Court said the first amendment right of a free press prevailed over the juvenile court's right of privacy. **If newspapers lawfully obtain the name and photographs of juveniles engaged in juvenile proceedings, they may publish them. Freedom of the press is more important than privacy for the juvenile.**[1]

Fare v. Michael C—1979

The Miranda warnings are given by police officers when an adult or juvenile is arrested, or taken into custody. Miranda warnings mean police officers have to tell a juvenile that anything the juvenile says can be used to convict the juvenile and the juvenile has a right to a defense lawyer even if the juvenile cannot afford to hire a lawyer. The state has to provide a free defense lawyer. If the juvenile asks for a defense lawyer, any questioning of the juvenile by the police has to stop until the defense lawyer shows up. This has been confirmed by other cases. **Juveniles have Miranda rights but can waive them; a request for a probation officer does not have the same status as a request for a lawyer. A request for a probation officer can be denied and the subsequent questioning can be used to prosecute the juvenile.**

Schall v. Martin, New York State—1984

Gregory Martin was arrested in New York City for robbery, assault and criminal possession of a weapon. He was arrested at 11:30 P. M. He gave a false address. He was detained and given an initial court appearance (arraignment) the next day with his grandmother present. The judge's reasons for detention were the lateness of the hour of the arrest, which showed lack of supervision, the loaded, gun and the false address. He ordered Gregory Martin detained before trial under NYS law 320, which provide preventive detention for juveniles.

Gregory Martin's lawyers created a class action case against preventive detention for all juveniles in New York State. The case was appealed to the US Supreme Court. Frankly, none of us would want Gregory on the street to prey on other human beings. However, if he had the right to bail, he most likely would have been denied bail for obvious reasons. However, the US Supreme Court said that there were enough procedural safeguards that preventive detention and the subsequent denial of all juvenile bail in the United States was constitutional. The court said basing preventive detention on the prediction of future wrongs of the juvenile was constitutional. **Preventative detention is constitutionally valid for juveniles. There is no right of bail or pretrial release for juveniles.**

New Jersey v. V.T.L.O.—1985

This is simply another example of the denial of adult constitutional rights to juveniles. There have been others including testing for drugs of juveniles by school authorities. As long as the court thinks any behavior is reasonable, all invasions of privacy of juveniles are constitutional including the schools forcing juveniles to be tested for drugs in their urine such as in Verona School District 471 v. Wayne and Judy Acton, ad litem Guardians for James Acton, 1995. **School authorities can institute searches without search warrants to preserve an environment conducive to education.**

Roper v. Simmons—2005

Stanford v. Kentucky and Wilks v. Missouri, 1989, stated that capital punishment for juveniles over the age of 16 years and older is constitutional and is not a cruel and unusual punishment. Wilks was sixteen and Stanford was seventeen when they committed the murder. Both were condemned to death, which is called capital punishment. The US Supreme Court decided that the states were free to impose the death penalty on juveniles ages 16 or 17.

In 2003, the Missouri Supreme Court decided that a consensus had formed that it was a cruel and unusual punishment to execute Juveniles under the age of 18. The U.S Supreme Court agreed to review the death penalty for 16 and 17 year olds. At that time 78 juveniles were on death row awaiting execution. From 1975–2003, 22 juveniles had been executed. Meanwhile the US Supreme Court had decided in Atkins v. Virginia, 2002, to abolish the death penalty for mentally retarded persons since the court felt that they were less responsible (culpable) for their actions. This set the precedent for abolishing the death penalty for juveniles ages 16 and 17. A further reason was what the courts cited as changing standards of decency since there was so few juveniles executed and some states had abolished the death penalty for those under age 18. The court did admit that Simmons had planned and carried out a murder at age 17 and that he had been sentenced to death. At the time 20 states sill imposed the death penalty on juveniles.

Simmons, age 17, planned the crime ahead of time, bound the woman, with a towel over her face, duct taped her face and threw her off a bridge. She drowned. He then bragged about the murder to his friends.

The court concluded that a consensus had developed making the execution of a person under the age of 18, a cruel and unusual punishment. The court did add that juveniles were immature, impulsive and susceptible to being influenced by their peers. **Under the eighth and fourteenth amendments forbidding cruel and unusual punishments, the death penalty for juveniles under the age of 18 was abolished.**

Juvenile Due Process Today

Juvenile and Family Courts are still civil courts and are not criminal courts. Juvenile courts are almost equivalent to adult criminal court due process.

The major exceptions are that Juvenile Courts provide:

- No right of public trial except in New York State.
- No right of a trial by jury.
- No right to bail or any other form of pretrial release. Juveniles may be held by force in preventive detention.
- Juveniles under 18 may not be executed.
- Juvenile court is a civil court and not a criminal court.

Confusion is caused by calling juvenile court a civil court with its adversarial proceedings and with criminal justice standards of reasonable doubt for evidence. Juvenile court can take away a juvenile's freedom for many years. Another issue is that juveniles can get longer sentences for minor crimes than they would get if they were tried in an adult criminal court. Juveniles also get sentenced for acts that would not be crimes if they were adults. Juvenile courts should be in the business of providing more protection for juveniles than for adults rather than taking away the juveniles' constitutional rights. Juvenile court still has a long way to go if it is to provide the equality before the law in court that adults enjoy.

The professionals in Juvenile Justice, lawyers, judges, probation officers, social workers, police and youth workers try their best to both protect the community and help troubled and criminal youth. In major metropolitan areas, the courts are under intense pressure from overwork and high caseloads. In some cities, the juvenile courts are close to self-destruction and mistakes are made. Outside of these areas, the courts take a more balanced and fair approach offering a variety of professional services and placements. Judges should have a minimum of five years of full time practice in juvenile and family courts. Finally the U.S. Supreme Court needs to give juveniles all the constitutional protections that adults have. Juveniles have a right to the constitutional protections of the Bill of Rights because they are citizens of the United States.

Juvenile Court Sentencing/Dispositions And Placements

Chapter Outline

Introduction

A Juvenile Court disposition is the same as sentencing in an adult criminal court. The language differs in different states but the meaning is the same. There is no guilty conviction in juvenile court since juvenile delinquency is not a crime. A fourteen-year-old may have murdered and robbed a person but if that juvenile were under the jurisdiction of juvenile court, the juvenile would be adjudicated a juvenile delinquent. If the juvenile is remanded to adult criminal court, then the juvenile could be convicted of murder and robbery, as an adult.

Adjudication is when the juvenile court judge makes a decision. The juvenile judge could decide to declare the juvenile not guilty and send the juvenile home. The judge's adjudication can also decide that the juvenile is guilty and, depending on age and the antisocial behavior, is either a person in need of supervision or a juvenile delinquent.

However, the language, guilty and not guilty is not used, confusing as this seems. The juvenile is never confronted with **guilty** even though this reality might help the juvenile deal with his or her behavior and its consequences. Once the juvenile is adjudicated, juvenile courts use either the disposition or sentencing language. Sentencing is easier to understand for most adults and juveniles, than disposition, so sentencing will be used from this point on.

Placement is another word that is used by the juvenile courts. For example, the juvenile could be placed with a family in foster care, in a group home or institutionalized behind locked doors. The juvenile could also be placed on probation. What actually happens to a juvenile for antisocial and criminal behavior is similar in the various states.

Major Considerations For Sentencing and Placement

—The age of the juvenile when the act took place.

—The seriousness of the antisocial behavior.

—The safety of the victim and the community.

—How responsible and supportive the parents or guardians are.

—If there is a bed available in an out-of-home placement.

—If the youth has special physical, sexual, mental or addictive treatment needs including various disabilities.

These are major factors for juvenile judges and probation officers. Parents and juvenile defense lawyers need to pay special attention to these factors if they wish to influence the outcome of the decision, including sentencing and placement.

Juvenile Court Sentencing/Dispositions

Adjournment in Contemplation of Dismissal

This is a juvenile court release for juveniles with a time period attached. The case is dismissed for a specific period of time, usually not more than six to twelve months for most states. During that time the court may order the juvenile to attend school, have a curfew, pay a cash restitution or do community service. If the juvenile gets into further trouble, the juvenile returns to court through *a petition for restoration* or similar language. The judge will be very unhappy with the juvenile, since the judge will normally feel that the judge gave the juvenile a chance to straighten out without further penalty. If all goes well and the juvenile straightens out, the case is dismissed at the end of the time period.

Conditional Discharge

An adjudicated juvenile is discharged at the end of a specific period of time, usually at the end of twelve months. There may be conditions, like a curfew, school attendance, etc. If the juvenile gets into trouble the juvenile is brought to court and may face revocation based on a violation hearing. The judge will again be unhappy with the juvenile since the judge will feel that the judge gave the juvenile a chance to straighten out. The judge may impose a more secure placement outside of the home and/or additional counseling to deal with the problems. If all goes well and the juvenile does not get into trouble, the juvenile is discharged, normally, into the custody of the juvenile's parents or guardian.

Suspended Judgment

This is the same as conditional discharge for juveniles who have been adjudicated PINS. Conditions are put in place. The sentence is usually for up to twelve months, with a revocation based on a violation hearing.

Probation

The adjudicated juvenile is placed on probation, in most states for one or two years, with a hearing for the second year in many jurisdictions. This may or may not include an out of home placement. The juvenile is discharged or released either at the end of the specific time period or the juvenile may have early discharge based on good behavior. The juvenile reports to a probation officer, which may include home, work and school visits. Conditions besides the ones already listed could include various forms of professional counseling including drug and alcohol abuse counseling. A revocation based on a violation hearing will bring the juvenile back to juvenile court for further sentencing by a juvenile judge.

Determinate Sentence

Juveniles are sentenced for a specific period of time, for example, one year. In many jurisdictions, the one-year can be extended to two years. In most jurisdictions there are no sentences beyond two years.

Indeterminate Sentence

The placement authorities or probation decide on the release or discharge time for the juvenile. However, the juvenile cannot, in most cases, be held beyond the age when the juvenile becomes legally an adult as determined by state law. In most jurisdictions, this would be the eighteenth birthday and/or the twenty-first birthday. The juvenile could be released before that date for good behavior.

The maximum sentence normally depends on when the juvenile is legally an adult in the state's criminal justice statutes. Juveniles have different ages to legally become an adult in the various states. The states have different ages to become an adult criminal, drive a vehicle, get married, drink alcoholic beverages, and become emancipated from parents and guardians and to vote.

Violation Hearing

Conditions are set and enforced by the court and probation for sentences. When the youth is documented as not carrying out these conditions such as a curfew or attending school, then a violation hearing is called for. The youth has a hearing before the juvenile judge in court including having a lawyer representing the juvenile. Facts are presented and the judge makes a decision. If these proceedings take place in juvenile court, as it often does, the juvenile judge decides if a violation of the sentence has taken place. Testimony may be taken from police, social workers, friends, family, witnesses and probation officers.

General Juvenile Court Placements

Juvenile Group Homes

Juvenile group homes consist most often of six to fifteen residents. The residents have to go to a public school or an alternate school. There is a need for a 24-hour day, 7-day week supervision. The level of security depends on the residents' risk to the community. Group homes need a long list of service workers and professionals. Some examples are supervisors, tutors, cooks, group counselors, and individual counselors. Roofs and plumbing need repair and altogether, it is an expensive project.

In most cases, community based group homes are not cost effective. They may become financially realistic when they are dedicated to an institutional placement or located on an institution's grounds. With the issues of security, group homes may become institutional prisons rather than community based institutions. These are the major criticisms. There has been an effort to place juvenile community group homes in middle class neighborhoods with middle class schools along with much middle class opposition. Middle class schools have a superior record of lack of violence. Their success rates in college placement are evident over lower class neighborhood schools.

Middle class neighborhoods have much less violence, crime and crack houses compared to lower class neighborhoods. These neighborhoods are more likely to have intact successful families with employed adults in legitimate jobs as role models. As the nation knows, adolescents do better in middle class neighborhoods. This is why, when people can afford it, parents and their children leave lower class neighborhoods to move to the suburbs. That is why adolescents do better in-group homes in middle class neighborhoods.

Foster Care

The basic concept of foster family homes is to have troubled juveniles taken care of by supportive families when the juveniles' families have failed in caring for these troubled youths. Foster care placement of juveniles by juvenile court has run from wonderful to degrading and horrible.

Reform programs and certification programs have been around the United States for as many years as there have been a foster home placement programs. They have helped. Any time a juvenile is placed in a foster care, parents, guardians, defense lawyers, and friends should look into the placement. They need to verify that basic food, clothing, shelter, counseling and schooling is provided. There is no substitute for this scrutiny.

Enriched foster care with tutoring and counseling services can be beneficial for both the foster care family and the juveniles in their care. All foster care parents need professional training. Just a few of the topics that need to be addressed for foster parent training are:

Foster Care Parent Training

- Dealing with aggressive behavior,
- Depression in juveniles,
- Use of psychotropic and addictive drugs,
- Sexual deviations,
- How to spot suicidal behavior and what to do according to the law,
- Juvenile law,
- General counseling techniques,
- Administering medicines and security for medicines,
- Privacy, confidentiality, criminal behavior and legal obligations,
- Juvenile alcoholism,
- Parenting skills,
- Positive listening skills,
- Teenage culture, the Internet and the use of cell phones.

These are minimum topics that need to be codified into the state licensing of foster parents as many states have done. More work needs to be done to provide specific standards and training for foster parents. There are also minimum standards for food, clothing, shelter and education.

Mental Health Placement

This is the most expensive placement in the system with the possible exception of 24-hour secure placement. Juvenile courts normally order mental health evaluation if there is any indication of severe neurotic or psychotic behavior. If the tests and evaluations show a mental health problem, then it up to state and court authorities to deal with these problems in the interests of protecting the community, the family and justice. This is a very serious and expensive obligation by the government and a major issue for the families involved with the juvenile. Counselors, psychologists and psychotherapists are engaged to deal with the juvenile in a mental health evaluation and placement. Expensive, professional therapy is needed and may take weeks, months and years to complete. However, this is the human condition and we should be grateful that America has the resources to deal with these major personal and social issues.

The Need For Alternate Schools

These give the delinquents a chance to learn and succeed with small group instruction (10–12 students). Teachers are trained to have an understanding of the obstacles these special education students need to overcome. It is often a necessary element in the successful integration of a delinquent back into the community.

Troubled youths are not disciplined, well-behaved students. Many have middle class goals of success but know that they have no legitimate means for these aspirations. As in other aspects of their delinquent life, including families that are drug and alcohol addicted and that lack adult family supervision, there is failure. Many of these delinquent youths have learning problems, fear of failure and the need to feel they are successful in front of their peers. Their friends are often motivated by violence and street values of confrontation. It takes specialized teachers and counselors to deal with these dreadful life issues. Intelligence is not an issue. Peer norms of violence and failure are the problem realities.

Many professionals grew up in these violent neighborhoods and never forget the lifestyle. The reality is part of your soul and your life. Other professionals have caseloads in the same neighborhoods and hear the echoes of the lifestyle for the rest of their personal and professional lives. Once you lived a life endangered, the rest of your life is centered in this reality. No one can ever avoid it, whatever they may say. This may seem dramatic but it is a reality that is part of street life, wherever that life may lead.

Electronic Homebound Detention

Youths wear a bracelet or anklet that cannot be taken off without setting off an alarm at probation or other facility. The youths are confined to their home with electronic measures except for work, school, office visits to a doctor or dentist, etc.

Institutionalization/Incarceration

This is an out-of-home placement that places a juvenile in a state or county facility that limits the freedom of the juvenile and provides schooling and counseling programs. It can be secure where the doors are locked and there are fencing and other walls around the facility or it can be non-secure where the juveniles can walk away. Normally the juveniles who have committed the most serious crimes are placed in secure facilities. They vary from being similar to college dorms to the most depressed and ugly institutions in the nation. These facilities need to be carefully monitored by official authorities in state government, the courts and the parents and guardians of incarcerated juveniles. This oversight should limit the documented ongoing abuse that takes place in these institutions nationally. One abusive institution is one too much. It is a sad commentary on our nation and our most vulnerable imprisoned delinquents. "Vigilance is the price of liberty" as Patrick Henry has told us. We need to protect our children by closely monitoring all juvenile institutions.

Conclusion

Communities offer a large mix of placements and programs for juveniles. Billions of dollars are spent but with little or no evaluations for most ongoing placements and programs. Realistically, we need a list of diverse programs that work for juveniles with various needs. More programs dedicated to specific needs in a juvenile delinquent's home neighborhood are desperately needed. More work needs to done with families rather than just the individual delinquent.

7

Counseling Juveniles

Chapter Outline

Introduction

We are including these short descriptions of counseling and therapeutic approaches to help the readers of *the Juvenile Justice Guide* understand what is happening to juveniles when professionals intervene in a juvenile's life. It may also help you, the reader, to ask the right questions to find out what is happening to the juveniles in custody. You can also use the Google web-based search program to find more information about these various approaches.

Besides general counseling textbooks and research, the authors sought out books that showed how counseling was used in the field with both adult criminals and delinquents. We have also interviewed many probation officers, juveniles and juvenile counselors. The following were especially useful for this chapter and the full citations can be found in the bibliography: Braswell, Fletcher and Miller, *Human Relations and Corrections*, Lester and Braswell, *Correctional Counseling*, Van Voorhis, Braswell and Lester, *Correctional Counseling and Rehabilitation*, Siegel, Welsh and Senna, *Juvenile Delinquency.*

Behavior Modification

This is used in some institutions to control the residents who are in custody. One approach is called the token or points system. Tokens or points awarded in order to make residents of institutions behave and do routine tasks such as making their bed. Behavior modification is based on the stimulus-response and reinforcement psychological model. Tokens and points reward the residents with increasing freedom of movement in the institution, extra visits home and extra desserts.

Eric Berne's Transactional Analysis

This approach to counseling has been popularized through gaming theory and a drama-like approach. Residents in therapy play different roles. In *Games People Play* there are three Psychological Roles played by patients. They are:

1. The **Parent** who is an authority figure who is in charge,
2. The **Child** is a dependent figure, who obeys the adult and plays subordinate games with the parent figure,
3. The **Adult** is a mature individual who is able to take responsibility for his or her actions.

Following is an example of games a juvenile might play in the I'm o.k. /Your o.k. language of the therapy.

> A Juvenile resident wants to get out of cleaning his room and tries to make his roommate responsible. He says, "It makes me depressed to clean my room." Translated: I am not o.k. and therefore can't clean my room. The counselor, who is an adult, says that every Friday morning all the residents clean their rooms. Your roommate will sweep the floor while you make the beds. You can both pick up and store your personal items. Then we will see a counselor about the depression. Translated: you are o.k. enough to clean your room. Resident: I will only do it if you order me to. Translated: I will only clean my room if you become a parent authority figure. Counselors: "If we are going to live here together we all have to pitch in." Translated: "I am an adult giving you a reason to be responsible." (Benes, 1971:22)

Carl Rogers' Nonjudgmental Therapeutic Approach

Reframing questions may help develop insight and a positive self-concept according to what has been called Rogerian Therapy named after Carl Rogers. For example, a juvenile says, "I like to pick a fight in school." The therapist rewords the statement without making judgments and says, "You like to pick fights." The therapist waits for a reaction from the juvenile. Most people do not do well with silence in a therapy session and usually continue talking on the subject. Rogerian therapy is often used to open up a juvenile in a non-threatening and positive manner. Juveniles genuinely feel better about themselves after experiencing a session with a Carl Roger's trained counselor. This approach doesn't work well with violence oriented street delinquents and habitual liars. This counseling lacks intervention strategies since no moral judgments are made about bad behavior. One of the criticisms is: if no judgment is made and stated when a juvenile says, "he likes to pick fights," this neutral stance might encourage the violent behavior. The object of the therapy is to change antisocial behavior. So therapy should not encourage antisocial behavior.

Family Therapy

Uses a systems approach to show the interaction of various family roles: treats the family and the client as part of an interacting unit. Family therapy works best when it incorporates parenting skills: consistent, warm, and affectionate with positive listening skills and anger-control techniques.

Guided Group Interaction

Guided Group Interaction is widely used and is at its best with a clinically trained group leader who stresses rules and boundaries for group interaction.

This approach can develop insight in learning to take responsibility for individual behavior as well as relate consequences to behavior. Shared experiences can help individuals learn how to manage their life better. Members of a group usually won't let other members of the group lie and deceive themselves and other members of the group. It also helps members of the group deal truthfully with their life styles. This approach needs a skilled counselor leader because if control of the group is lacking, destructive individuals who are members of the group will attack each other and the leader will be looking for emotional weak spots.

William Glasser's Reality Therapy

This approach teaches us that each youth is responsible for his or her own behavior. The therapist does not accept excuses for bad behavior like unconscious motivation, family background, victimization, or living in a bad neighborhood.

"This is the first day of your life." Approach stresses positive change and the ability of each juvenile to have a successful life. Therapy begins with a realistic appraisal of the client's reality and then plans for the future. The therapist makes moral judgments, and rejects immoral behavior.

Reality therapy is based on realistic judgments and honesty.

Reality therapy techniques include:

- involvement,
- the rejection of irresponsible behavior and
- the teaching of better behavior.

Both the therapist and the juvenile client take responsibility for their behavior. With a realistic judgment on their present status, their strengths and weaknesses, plans can now be made for a more positive future. (http://www.wglasser.com/)

Milieu Therapy

Milieu therapy involves every member of the staff in a residence in therapy including such people and the cooks and janitors. Opening up your innermost feelings with total honesty, communication and listening skills are emphasized to immerse the client totally in the community 24 hours a day, 7 days a week. Therapy is continual with everyone involved—all the staff and all the residents—all the time. This was used more in the past. However, aspects of milieu therapy are often part of group living in juvenile facilities.

Psychodrama

This is where clients play the roles of significant people in their lives, mother, father, spouse, best friend, enemies, etc. The audience is part of the play and the therapist can be a player. Roles are switched continually with clients playing themselves, and then switching to becoming the mother or father, or victim. Although this approach develops deep insight, it needs to be carefully controlled by a well-trained therapist with a great deal of experience. Psychodrama is intense and emotionally draining. Erving Goffman of Harvard created an approach to these social roles, which has been called dramaturgy, where he talks about role-playing in real life.

Psychological Classifications and "I" Levels

This has been used to classify clients in both residential and community-based programs based on maturity level, levels of morality and introvert/extrovert classifications for many years. "I" levels has been used as a basis for further therapy. Psychological testing of the juveniles is often used to place them under the appropriate maturity levels and recommend specific counseling approach.

Marguerite Q. Warren wanted a classification system that showed that all offenders were not alike (Warren: 1971) so she devised a system, which would identify differences for juvenile offenders. She identified asocial offenders who had no social values and aggressive and passive offenders. She identified the manipulator who used people, and the conformist. Adolescent offenders had to include immature offenders. She also included the psychological standard of neurotics who were deviant but still functioning socially. Finally she devised a cultural conformist who identified with their friends and peers, that was especially made for delinquent gangs. Her usual recommendation was counseling in the community along with the specifics that matched her profile of the delinquent's personality. The amoral delinquent would respond to power and a command system while the delinquents with values could be dealt with through counseling.

The Role of the Counselor/
Therapist in Juvenile Institutions

The workday includes an incredible variety of work, intensive organization and a great deal of bureaucratic paper work. Being conned is a major element of the workday. A major ethical dilemma is the confidentially of the client and protecting the community, the institution and upholding the law. Counselors, by law, have to report present, past and any future crimes to the proper legal authorities. Yet, counseling is said to work best when there is confidentiality, which builds trust between the client and the therapist. This can be a real conflict of interest. Attorney-Client privileges are stricter in protecting confidentiality unless a life is threatened.

The client-centered, helping professional often has the power to recommend punishments, confinement and loss of privileges in a juvenile institution. In a community setting, this could include arrest and incarceration. This often results in a conflict of interest in a therapeutic setting where the counselors are there to help the youths have better lives. The law is clear. Counselors, in a juvenile institution, must report all past, present and future crimes to the proper authorities. If a juvenile tells a counselor that other juveniles are taking heroin, immediate action must be taken. It would be irresponsible and illegal to not take action.

Interviewing Juveniles

The interview process becomes engaged in two major areas when an individual becomes involved in the juvenile justice system, at the intake stage and the presentence stage for a probation agency. Social services and police agencies also interview juveniles.

A juvenile is sentenced to probation or various forms of institutionalization by the judge in Juvenile Court. Interviews are significant factors in recommending to a sentencing judge, secure institutionalization, group homes, foster care or going back home with counseling. Of course, there are many other factors such as the difference between murder and skipping school. Interviews and the documentation of interviews with juvenile are important throughout the juvenile justice process. What a juvenile reveals, documents and confesses to at every interview, effects what will happen to the juvenile. All interviews are important no matter how casual they may seem. Interviews are used to document the case, supervision of the juvenile, violations and placements, to name just a few significant events in a juvenile's life under the justice system.

Interviewers need a context to understand the background, life style, family and neighborhood of the juvenile. A look at the criminal history helps. This leads to an understanding of the juvenile's truthfulness. Official documentation is essential as is the contextual record. The interviewer has to judge whether the juvenile is admitting past and present offenses, minimizing these offenses or lying.

Using this background and criminal history knowledge, the interviewer can easily take charge of the interview. This take-charge attitude is essential to a successful interview. Interviewers, for the most part, need to be direct and assertive in their questioning of juveniles. Whatever the juveniles' crimes and sophistication, these juveniles are still adolescents with an adolescent mind set and psychology.

Probation officers, as interviewers, need to spell out the exact rules of supervision and sentences of probation. This includes the rules and expectations concerning a violation of probation. All of these rules need to be in writing and handed to both the juvenile and the juvenile's family. It is necessary to document everything in case this documentation is needed for a violation of probation hearing.

Techniques are important from the direct question to all follow-up questions, including facts that can be documented and emotional responses. The interview starts with easily answered questions such as name, address, family members, and the juvenile's alias or street name, like Juice or Grease. Criminal history is always compared to the official record and the current offense to the arrest report. A certain rhythm is created, a sense of give and take. Interviewers need to pay special attention to deceptive statements and contradictions. The goals of these interviews is to provide the best placement and counseling for the juvenile and protect the community.

A Final Note On Confidentiality and Conflict of Interest

Psychologists, psychotherapists, social workers and counselors have strong professional rules about not talking about a client's therapy and keeping what a client says confidential. When joining professional associations, they agree to a code of ethics, which includes keeping counseling sessions confidential. Violation of this professional rule is considered unethical. These rules of confidentiality are normally not protected by law in the same way the lawyer-client privilege is.

The law expects under penalty of law, up to and including felonies, that knowledge of a crime that has taken place or will take place be reported to the courts or the police. If a juvenile, in counseling or therapy, talks about drug use in an institution or even on the street, the counselor is expected to report this information to the legal authorities. In a juvenile institution *not reporting* drug use by residents, will put other residents at risk. Not reporting illegal drug use would be considered unprofessional behavior, grounds on which to fire an employee and for legal prosecution by the district attorney. For criminal justice professionals, the ethical and legal rule is to report all criminal activity and any behavior that would place another juvenile or adult in harm's way. Anything less than this is considered unethical, unprofessional and illegal. This would include illegal drugs. It also includes any adult, male or female, employed by the institution that sexually preys upon the male or female juveniles. Covering up these crimes is also illegal and considered a broach of trust in protecting the juveniles from harm.

This dilemma is normally dealt with by telling counseling and therapy clients before any counseling or therapy takes place, that anything the clients say about past and future crimes or putting any citizen or client at risk will be reported to the counselor's superiors and the legal authorities, including the police. By informing the clients, these professionals feel that they have ethically resolved any issue between their professional ethics and the law. In all other instances, normal confidentiality is kept.

Conclusion

The counseling and interview approaches to helping troubled youth and juveniles have proven useful over time. Any one approach would be determined by the needs, circumstances and personality of the juvenile. A professional counselor has the education, training and clinical experience to try a variety of approaches until one works better than others. This is not a random approach. A judgment is made based on interviews, psychological testing and the knowledge of how to interpret these evaluations and tests. It is a long involved process by an experienced and highly educated counseling professional. This is how it should be done.

Never hesitate to ask the background, education, training and licensing of any professional involved in intervention activities and the counseling of juveniles. This is not a job for amateurs because amateurs can do more harm than good. There are few empirical evaluations of any of these approaches, but they have been used for many years with many successful outcomes.

Juvenile Delinquency Theories

Chapter Outline

Introduction

This is a summary of the major theories in juvenile justice and delinquency that try to explain why juveniles commit crime other than antisocial behaviors. Some of the theories have been documented empirically more than others. These theories are being taught in college juvenile justice and juvenile delinquency courses throughout the United States and the world. Only theories that explain juvenile behavior directly are used. Marxist/Conflict theory, for example, has little explanatory power concerning actual juvenile behavior, so we are not concerned with it. The labeling hypothesis, which has been widely believed by juvenile justice court personnel, has never been proven. The labeling hypothesis states that if you label a juvenile as a bad person this will result in antisocial and criminal behavior. Juvenile courts have been closed to the public and juvenile names have been hidden from public disclosure based on this unproven hypothesis. It is unfortunate, but the labeling hypothesis is pure nonsense.

Let us now examine a summary of those theories that make more sense and do explain some juvenile antisocial behavior. The people who created these theories were, in general, sociology professors who published books and articles in scholarly journals. General theory books and individual books by the many scholars cited in this chapter are in our extensive bibliography.

Control Theory

Control Theory assumes that people are aggressive with a potential for violence and need to be controlled through social bonding to legitimate social institutions including school, community, church, legitimate peers and family. A further assumption is that the middle class morality of respect for property and people with basic honesty in word and deed is the only legitimate morality for human beings.

This includes self-defense if attacked but otherwise control theory assumes a need to preserve a peaceful community and lifestyle. This is a consensus model of community values and includes a goal of protecting individuals and the community from those who wish to violate the middle class rules.

Jackson Toby's Stake In Conformity

- Peer support
- How well the youth did in school
- The need of support from home and community

This early approach stressed traditional middle class values and makes a great deal of sense. Adolescents need to succeed in school to feel good about themselves. The need support from friends, family and the community stressing what was called then, legitimate values. There hasn't been a great deal of change concerning these values from the 1950's to the present.

Control Theory by Travis Hirschi

(a Sociologist, way back in 1969), included:

- Attachment — to parents, conventional peers and doing well in school
- Commitment — to lawful careers, educational and occupational aspirations
- Involvement — in conventional activities
- Belief — in conventional rules, for example, respect for the law

---

Early Control theory research did not focus on serious delinquent youth but instead focused on minor deviance like skipping school or occasionally stealing small sums of money. Inciardi's study of serious delinquent youths in Miami, 1985–87, which included violent drug dealers and Sherman's study of misdemeanor family violence and police arrests in 1992, recommend control theory for its explanatory value of their research. (Both Inciardi and Sherman have published extensively in the field of criminal justice and are well-known scholars.) The more recent social development model uses control theory when the theory focuses on the development of pro-social bonds by juveniles. Control theory is being used widely in current research projects and for the creation of integrated criminological theories.

Choice Theories

Choice Theory assumes that criminals and delinquents will make rational cost/benefit decisions based on personal gain (pleasure) and personal losses (pain). This is in the tradition of the 19th century utilitarian British philosophers Jeremy Bentham and John Stuart Mill. John Stuart Mill added a civil liberties notion that anything not forbidden by government is obviously permitted, as he stated in his essay, "On Liberty". He added that, anything that does not directly harm another human should be permitted. He also stated that qualitative pleasure could overcome the hedonic calculus of Mr. Bentham. A major issue is that the pleasure of the many may overwhelm the pain of the few. For example, the smell of a rose may overwhelm the stench of an Asian prison. The rational conclusion becomes: if there is more to gain than to lose, the criminal will commit the crime.

Becarria defined the pleasure principle for justice in a logical manner—the cost/benefit decision. Based on that principle, punishment should be swift, near the time of the crime and sure, with 100% certainty. Current studies of the punishment of children confirm this approach. The logical approach to punishment also argues that the government should use the least punishment to stop people from committing the crime.

To apply Becarria's methods, one would use:

1. The rational cost/benefit approach
2. Swift and sure punishment
3. The least punishment needed to stop recidivism.

Routine Activities Theory: You also need to engage in target hardening such as the use of burglar alarms and high tech locks. As we go about our daily activities, we make choices, which helps criminals or hinders criminals from victimizing us. Following is a list of those choices.

1. We can travel with **capable guardians** such as friends that can protect us or hang out as loners in strange bars late at night.
2. We can have good locks on our doors and windows or we can make it easier for criminals to burglarize our homes by leaving the doors open and talking about our coin collection with strangers. People often leave their sliding glass patio doors unsecured. Juvenile use these lapses for daylight burglary and many owners do not even know they have been burglarized. Don't you remember that valuable ring you misplaced? It was stolen by a neighborhood teenager. Keeping our homes safe is **target hardening**.
3. We can avoid **motivated offenders** or hang out with them. Lower class neighborhoods often have large number of unemployed males. A certain number these males are motivated to make their living through mugging and robbery. We should avoid these males. For example, an older man *routinely* cashed his pension check at a neigh-

borhood store and walked home with the cash in his back pocket. He was mugged, and killed when he entered his apartment.

4. **Defensible space** is part of situational crime prevention such as well-lighted streets and lighted public housing. The extensive use of surveillance cameras such as those being installed in the New York City subways and neighborhood crime patrols help create safe space that is defended from criminal predators.

Differential Association

Differential Association by Edwin Sutherland is one of the first widely accepted theories with the promise of empirical and behavioral evidence to back it up. Although the evidence never materialized, this theory ended the so-called "armchair" theories of speculation. Scholars generally agreed with Edwin Sutherland, that delinquent behavior is learned through being exposed to criminal norms in intimate groups of friends and family called primary groups. Norms are cultural and sub-cultural guides to action. A more modern approach uses exposure to criminal behavior rather than norms.

This is a **learning theory** approach where delinquents learn through verbal and nonverbal communication definitions of legal codes as favorable or unfavorable.

Delinquent behavior is learned in primary groups of friends, family and small groups at work and school involving all the mechanisms of learning using both verbal and nonverbal communications. The earlier a youth is exposed to criminal norms, the more frequent the youth comes into contact with criminal norms and the more intensive the interaction, the more likely the youth is to be involved in criminal behavior. An excessive exposure to criminal and delinquent norms compared to exposure to legitimate legal norms, means you are more likely to become a delinquent.

Differential association makes sense and has fascinated scholars for decades but is largely unproven. Once again, if your friends and family are criminals and delinquents, it makes sense that you will more likely become involved in criminal and delinquent behavior.

When a youth accepts an excess of norms unfavorable to legal behavior, the result is antisocial delinquent behavior such as believing it is all right to steal. The earlier you learn the criminal norms in life and the more frequent and the more intense the exposure to criminal norms, the more likely a youth will become delinquent. Differential Association is popular but has almost no believable proof that it works. However, it does make sense if your friends and family are involved in criminal activities, that the children as they grow up are more likely to become delinquent. By rejecting the genetic (inheritance) approach, differential association led the way to theories based on scientific evidence.

Strain Theory

Strain Theory says that if a juvenile accepts standard American goals but innovates alternate illegitimate means to reach these goals such as stealing, they are more likely to become delinquent. This is where the strain takes place. You want a nice house and car in a good neighborhood where you can support your spouse and children, but you steal to obtain this legitimate life style.

Robert Merton, a Harvard Sociologist, in 1938 published an article that has dominated a good deal of thinking about crime and delinquency. There were what he called **cultural goals**, which were the standard middle class American goals of achievement, that by working hard and getting rewarded for that work, Americans would earn a middle class life style.

American Middle Class Cultural Goals

1. Owning a middle class house or living in a nice apartment
2. Living in a safe, well-maintained neighborhood
3. More than adequate safety and a high quality diet
4. Nice clothes to wear for all weather for the whole family
5. A good school for the children to learn successful skills
6. Affordable and decent medical and dental care
7. Owning nice cars for all members of the family
8. A decent middle class retirement.

This is a pretty good way to live and most of the world aspires to this life style. There are also the middle class values of respecting other people's property and persons and telling the truth. The middle class is against stealing, lying, assault, killing and cheating, and American laws generally reflect these values.

The **institutional means** for achieving this good life includes the American Rule of Law and affordable educational opportunities. What Americans want is to work hard and succeed in a good school. Be successful in a good job. The reward would be a middle class life style.

It is necessary to defer some gratification to reach these middle class cultural goals. Grandparents, parents and youth need to save for college costs and work hard to do this. American youths must continue to work hard in the classroom in business and professional schools without an immediate payoff. These American youths do expect a future payoff in terms of the American cultural goal of a middle class life style for both themselves and their children. With the lack of affordable health care and good jobs going to underclass third world countries, which are sponsored by American global corporations, these middle class goals are becoming harder to achieve.

A major psychological characteristic of delinquent youth is immediate gratification, no matter what the cost. Middle class youths defer gratification while going to college while delinquent youths steal to have money to buy clothes and cars. This is one reason delinquent youths commit property crimes.

Some people who rejected the middle class institutional means to achieve these goals or did not have these means available to them would **innovate**. For example, they would steal rather than work in a middle class job. Dealing drugs, stealing and using violence to achieve a middle class lifestyle is typical of criminal and delinquent behavior. Many of the corporate and banking middle and upper class use fraudulent behavior to steal and to violate middle class ethics (class norms) but are protected by power, money and weak laws.

Robert Merton's Strain Theory Chart

"Types of Adaptation by Individuals Within A Culture Bearing Society"

Modes of Adaptation		Culture Goals	Institutional Means
I	Conformity	Accepted	Accepted
II	Innovation	Accepted	Rejected
III	Ritualism	Rejected	Accepted
IV	Retreats	Rejected	Rejected
V	Rebellion	Current Cultural Goals Rejected	Current Institutional Means Rejected
		New Cultural Goals Created	New Institutional Means Created

Conformity is when you accept the cultural goal of the good life and you have legitimate means to reach that goal like going to college and being hired in a good job with benefits.

Innovation is when you want the good life but you either don't have the means to obtain it or you reject the legitimate means. For example, rather than getting a steady job, you become a drug dealer in order to earn the down payment for your house in the suburbs. Another way to innovate is to drop out of college and invent something like Apple Computer or Microsoft.

Ritualism is when you simply do not want the cultural goals of the good life, or equal justice for all, but you really like and accept the institutional means. People who go to church or temple, and don't believe in the goals of the religion, are ritualistic. Administrators who don't care about graduating students, but want everyone to obey all the rules all the time, seem to be one of the most frustrating ritualistic types.

Retreat is when you reject the legitimate means and goals of middle class society and retreat from society. Some alcoholics, drug addicts and homeless people may be considered retreating from life.

Rebellion can take in the whole society with a social revolution or become a counterculture or a deviant subculture. From the 1960's through the present, young people have founded intentional communities, which were based on Utopian principles, which included many American values with a lifestyle of group living that was very different.

"Ecological" Neighborhood Theories and Counter-Cultures

Ecological in this context means that the theorist takes in all aspects of a neighborhood, such as amount of crime, quality of the schools, church programs, types of families, unemployment, illegal drug use, and alcoholism.

Gresham Sykes and David Matza in the 1950's based their study on interviews with a small number of boys. They discovered that these boys seemed to believe in middle class values but constantly violated the law.

They discovered that these boys made up excuses to justify the law violations. The question, which intrigued them, is: "Why do these boys violate the law that they seemed to believe in." They found that:

1. Most boys are not hardened criminals.
2. The boys admire law-abiding people as role models.
3. Some delinquents do experience guilt and shame.
4. The delinquents they studied, determined who were victimized based on social distance.

Social distance is how close the boys felt to a person: going from their immediate family compared to distant strangers. For example, the boys would steal from a store but not from a close friend's family.

Techniques of Neutralization

1. **Denial of Responsibility**, "I didn't mean it."

   A boy beats another boy and breaks his arm. The reason would be that it was an accident or because he was brought up in a bad neighborhood. He could say the cause of his bad behavior was because he had been victimized: been abused by his mother as a child. His excuse is he broke that boy's arm because his mother made him do it. His prior victimization becomes an excuse for his present bad and violent behavior.

2. **Denial of Injury.** "I didn't really hurt anybody."

3. **Denial of Victim.** "They had it coming to them."

4. **Condemnation of the Condemners.** "Everybody's picking on me, especially the police, the probation officer, my parents or my teachers."

5. **Appeal to Higher Loyalties.** "I didn't do it for myself. I did it for my friends or for my gang."

Differential Opportunity by Cloward and Ohlin described how the availability of illegitimate means, in crime neighborhood, showed adult criminals teaching delinquent youth criminal skills and opportunities to commit crime.

Miller's Focal Concerns documented a male counter-culture made up of the following values: looking for trouble, toughness, smartness, excitement, fate, and a high need for autonomy. These generally went against middle class values.

Socially Disorganized Neighborhoods is also called an ecological approach. This theory shows delinquency as well organized responsive group behavior, where successive generation of racial and ethnic groups pass through a crime-dominated and socially disorganized neighborhood. Disorganization means that social institutions such as the family, the church and the school are failed institutions. Professors Shaw and McKay did the original study in Chicago over many years with no published empirical proof. Subsequent studies showed that growing up in a lower class neighborhood with drug and violence problems, and a large percent of unemployed males and single mothers put adolescent boys and girls at a high risk for delinquency (Wright and Wright, among others). Other studies have shown that the black families in these neighborhoods were socially well organized with a network of friends and relatives supporting them. (Giddens, et al. 2003:478–480)

It makes sense that if your neighborhood is full of crime, illegal drugs, poor schools, alcoholism, unemployed males and single mothers, that you are more at risk to become a delinquent. Accepting antisocial values and norms where there is a lack of legitimate jobs and many criminal opportunities will, of course, make the youth more at risk for delinquency.

Juvenile Gangs

Gangs are different than friends hanging out, dating together and enjoying each other's company. Gangs are criminal enterprises that have been created, for example, to steal, sell illegal drugs and intimidate citizens by threatening them with violence (Knox, 1994:7). Youth gangs have been around for over a hundred years in the United States. The largest youth gang in New York City at the beginning of the twentieth century was the Dead Rabbits, which ruled the streets around the five corners in Manhattan and were extremely violent. This historical street corner is still there as documented many years ago in *The Gangs of New York* and the recent movie. Juvenile gangs can stand alone or be affiliated with adult gangs. They go all the way from being loosely organized in a neighborhood, to having affiliates nationwide and in foreign countries with written rules and constitutions. Some theorists have said that gangs are substitutes for dysfunctional families where adolescents can develop parent substitutes and be protected from a violent neighborhood. Many juvenile gangs are simply there to make money illegally.

Today, there are separate female gangs. In the past, most females were associated with male gangs but did not have full and equal gang membership. Since then, savvy and tough females have risen to leadership roles and are full members of gangs. Many male gangs are chauvinistic as can be seen from rap songs that glorify machismo, illegal drugs, rape and violence and demean females. Female gang members are becoming more violent and less submissive to the males.

Gangs have rituals, colors, turf and symbols to unify gang memberships. Older members recruit younger ones and they generally have a home turf in a lower class neighborhood. Some examples of counterculture gangs are the CRIPS and the Bloods, the Vice Lords, the Blackstone Rangers, the Latin Kings, the Black Guerilla Family, The Mexican Mafia, The Russian Mafia and the Black Gangster Disciples. Gangs are often built around an ethnic identity, for example, African American gangs, Asian gangs; white gangs affiliated with hate groups and Hispanic gangs from various countries in Central America and Mexico. It would be easy to list hundreds of others. Most are located in urban decay areas, although some have branched out to small towns and rural areas to distribute illegal drugs. Organized crime and drug cartels are global in structure. Gangs have also become global, in part, based on the millions of illegal and undocumented immigrants living in the United States and the increased use of global information technology.

The most successful approach to diminishing gang violence starting with the Boston Gun Project has been a team approach of local, state and federal prosecutors, law enforcement personnel and community correction authorities with relentless prosecution. These authorities using a variety of state and federal laws take the leaders, and most violent members of these gangs, off the street and incarcerate them for as many years as they can. With violent gangs, social work intervention, high school programs and counseling simply doesn't work. Over the years most of the members of violent gangs either end up in prison as young adults or are killed in the streets by other gang members (Kennedy, 1998, Office of Juvenile Justice and Delinquency Prevention, 1999). One reporter visited a South side Chicago youth gang that he had written a book on twenty years previously, and found roughly three living members who were not dead or in prison.

Psychological and Biological Trait Theory and Genetic Approaches to Delinquent Behavior

The earliest approaches were based on genetic inheritance of criminal and physical traits. Lombroso (1835–1909), an Italian with medical training used empirical measurement of sentenced criminals compared to various groups of non-criminal and came up with a criminal physical type. Criminologists who made more accurate measurements but never proved their case empirically followed him. The best known were Ferri (1856–1929), Goring's (1870–1919) inheriting physical criminal tendencies (criminal diathesis), and Hooton (1930's) along with various twin and adoption studies. XYY Chromosome has no relevance to delinquents but tried to explain some violent behavior. Genetic research on alcohol dependency, diabetes, addictive personality, schizophrenia, and manic depression has a marginal relevance to delinquency but no trustworthy empirical evidence. The body types of Sheldon in the 1940's and Glueck and Glueck in the 1950's have very little relevance today. The Gluecks showed a muscular youth would more likely be a delinquent and identified certain psychological traits of delinquents that may be useful such as a need for immediate gratification—"I want it now!" Middle class non-delinquents defer gratification, for example, by working hard to get good grades in high school and going to college in order to have a future legitimate career.

The Antisocial Personality

- Immediate gratification
- Impulsive
- Egocentric
- No feeling of right from wrong in terms of middle class standards
  - —Counterculture morality against middle class standards
  - —Aggressive
  - —Low anger control
  - —Lack of empathy
  - —Poor social skills

This is drawn from a variety of sources, mostly descriptive studies and case histories. The Diagnostic and Statistical Manual of Mental Disorders (DSM), which uses the same language, was created by the American Psychiatric Association to collect insurance money for mental health professionals. The bloated manual all too often changes ordinary behavior to mental disorders and has little relevance to the actual behavior of delinquents in real life. In the past the association has made homosexuality into a mental disorder and it has also made shyness into a mental disorder. Various forms of delinquency and antisocial behavior have also been made into mental disorders. Some of this behavior was called conduct disorders. Sociologists have considered what would be a normal responsive to living in a violent, lower class neighborhood with high unemployment and an active illegal drug culture. The DSM would consider many of the responses as a mental disorder. Normal life has its ups and downs and this is not a sign of a mental disorder. The original Volume One of the DSM related mental disorders to specific behaviors and was a useful tool for counseling.

Adolescence and Delinquency

Adolescence is basically the teen-age years in junior high school and high school. These are the years when youths experience an identity crisis and they are trying to establish an adult identity mixed together with puberty and dealing with their maturing sexuality. The girls mature faster than the boys emotionally while all are experiencing awkwardness as their bodies mature. Their peer group of friends is very important to them, reflected in adolescent dress and values. As a group, adolescents are other-directed rather than inner-directed.

With all the hormonal, emotional and physical changes, these youths have a profound need for stability, safety and consistent rules and routines in their lives.

Family disorganization creates a high risk for delinquency. Adolescents, with their need for security, have an intolerance of differences such as a high school student from a different culture or neighborhood. They are also learning both pro-social and antisocial norms through play, sports, and social cooperation within the home and on the playing field. By arguing and discussing rules in sport games, for example, these adolescent youths gain a feeling for justice, fair play and leadership.

This is a period when these youths form adolescent subcultures, including friendship groups, clubs and antisocial gangs. They can learn values through socialization for the middle class or learn counter cultures values, which reject middle class values and norms. During this time, and this process, there is a great deal of rebellion against authority figures such as parents and school authorities.

Tasks of the Adolescent Years

1. Learning to work, use tools and prepare for an economic career. This includes becoming computer literate and using technology.
2. Achieving a gender identity, preparing for family life
3. Achieving mature gender relations
4. Learning social control and the middle class goal of responsible behavior
5. Learning to use the changing body effectively
6. Achieving emotional independence
7. Socialization tasks: learning a consistent set of basic values and norms
8. Learning self-respect and to like yourself
9. Learning empathy and emotional maturity
10. Cognitive development and the manipulation of abstract concepts along with speech and social communication skills. These skills are especially needed in high

---

> school achievement and our mature technological society based on information technology (IT).
>
> If these tasks are not successfully completed then the adolescent is at high risk for delinquency. If these tasks are completed in terms of counterculture values and norms, including gang behavior, then the adolescent will most likely engage in delinquent behavior. Successful completion of these tasks will result in a mature adult and a contributing member of society.

Life Course Theory and Other Integrated Theories

Over the last two decades, delinquency scholars have bundled older sociological and psychological theories into what have been called integrated theories. They have also engaged in empirical research in major cities and usually have confirmed their various descriptions of delinquents. They have brought together social learning theories, delinquency personality traits, criminal neighborhoods and the influence of an antisocial v. a pro-social family and friends. Pro-social means that family and friends believe in middle class values such as respecting other people's property and persons, so youths are less likely to steal and beat people up. This was called bonding and attachment to legitimate family and friends in control theory. The language describing antisocial delinquent behaviors has changed for the 21st century while the behaviors remain pretty much the same.

Most delinquency occurs as youths are maturing during the adolescent years as teenagers. Researchers have been interested in youths who stopped criminal behavior after adolescence compared to youths who continued criminal activity as adults. A small percentage of adolescents become adult criminals. Inciardi in his empirical study, *Street Kids, Street Drugs and Street Crime* stated that roughly eight per cent (8%) of what he called "garden variety" less serious delinquents, become serious delinquents, what various studies have called recidivist delinquents (Inciardi, 1993, Siegel, Welsh and Senna, 2006: 142-171, chapter on "Developmental Views of Delinquency) and Piquero and Mazrolle, *Life-Course Criminology*, 2001). One researcher used the language of "adolescent-limited v. life-course persisters" (Siegel, Welsh and Senna, 2006:147).

For a very good description of the various integrated theories and the wide variety of factors cited as reasons that youths become delinquents, see the Siegel, Welsh and Senna textbook in its many editions. These factors have all been described throughout the *Juvenile Justice Handbook*.

Once again, if young people who are maturing into adulthood and

1. live with a disorganized disruptive family that does not supervise them adequately,
2. in a lower class neighborhood that has criminal and illegal drug activity with a high unemployment of males,
3. with these juveniles developing at-risk personality characteristics such as a need for immediate gratification, and aggressive behavior . . .

then these youths are at high risk for delinquency.

For youths that move into or live in middle class neighborhoods with stable families, these risk factors diminish dramatically. Most of the risk factors and theories explaining delinquency make sense. Parents, police, probation officers, youth workers and juvenile judgers need to be aware of the factors that place youths at risk for delinquent behavior.

CHAPTER

9

What Works For Juveniles

Chapter Outline

Introduction

This is a general survey and brief description of specific programs and approaches, from both the past and present that have helped juveniles deal with their problems and/or reduced delinquency. A few widely-used programs that have not worked will also be reviewed. Overall, this will be a positive approach. There is a wide variation in the scientific evaluation of these programs. In order to make this chapter useful, statistical analysis and other technical language will be avoided. A bibliography will be provided with short descriptions of the most useful sources and references.

Parenting and Neighborhoods

Children and youths grow up in families in many different neighborhoods. The family, two parents, single parent or foster family dominates a child's life. Families need to love their children and set adult boundaries for children and adolescents. Parents and guardians need to provide the necessary supervision so that children and youths can live up to adult rules and standards. Neighborhoods need to be safe with guardian and role models who believe in middle class rules of honesty and civility. Besides basic needs of food, clothing, shelter and schooling, this is the minimum needed to protect children and adolescents from delinquent behavior.

Supervision

Supervision is the key element in successful parenting according to the research.

Two parents rather than one parent families provide more supervision so that adolescents are less likely to get into trouble in lower class neighborhoods with an excess of single mothers and unemployed males. Compared to lower class neighborhoods, middle class neighborhoods have less street drugs, violent behavior both inside and outside of the home and LESS criminal behavior in the streets. Middle class neighborhoods and schools have more volunteer guardians such as neighbors who are willing to intervene to provide middle class boundaries for children and youths. (Wright and Wright, 1995)

The cost of *not supervising children* and youths is encouraging both lower class and middle class delinquency among the unsupervised youths. Middle class delinquency is more likely to involve shoplifting, alcohol and marijuana drug abuse. Lower class delinquency will involve harder drug use such as heroin, violence and serious property crimes such as armed robbery. Cocaine, in its various forms, has a high appeal for all social classes. A lower class neighborhood will provide more opportunity to get involved in violence, drugs and crime. Criminal adult role models are more apt to be available in lower class neighborhoods. Criminal adults and juvenile gangs teach criminal skills to juveniles in these neighborhoods. Middle class parents can afford to hire middle class baby sitters and other enforcers of middle class norms. More guardians are available to supervise youths in middle class neighborhoods. Lower class parents simply do not have the economic resources to hire middle class supervision for their children. All of the ecological neighborhood theories and data confirm this as well as day-to-day newspaper stories. (Siegel, Welsh and Senna, 2006, Vold, et al., 2001)

Parental Training and Skills

If parents are emotionally cold and indifferent to their children with lax discipline, adolescents will rebel and end up with delinquent behavior. This includes aggressiveness and criminal behavior for boys, while the girls are more likely to run away and engage in early sexual adventures. If parents are lax in enforcing middle class norms, adolescents will *not know* the difference between right and wrong. Research indicates that the most important behavior of parents is *consistency* concerning rules and boundaries for children and adolescents. Inconsistency means that children believe that there is no relationship between behavior and rewards and punishments. Parents need to provide love, affection and boundaries of acceptable behavior. Consistency and emotional support with proportional punishments show that there are consequences for behavior. Cold and indifferent parents with strong rules will develop anxious and sullen children. A permissive parent with little or no rules and boundaries will have spoiled children. These juveniles will be self-confident and socially aware but they will also bend rules and feel they do not have to obey rules. Warm, loving parents who teach children to respect reasonable rules that are consistently enforced will produce children who are civil, value adult approval and obey the law.

Following is a scenario of inconsistent rule enforcement by the parent or parents. The parent sets an 8:00 P.M. deadline to be home on school days. The following happens. The juvenile has to be told what the specific punishment would be for breaking the rule. The best approach is when the parent and juvenile can agree on what would be an appropriate punishment. *Grounding a juvenile in the juvenile's room after school to supper, with no computer, and any cell or landline phone use for an appropriate number of days would work for many juveniles.*

Time That the Juvenile Comes Home		Inconsistent Parental Action
Monday	9:00	Juvenile is punished
Tuesday	7:30	Parent is angry and punishes juvenile
Wednesday	10:00	Parent ignores juvenile. No punishment
Thursday	8:00	Parent praises juvenile
Friday	8:30	Parent punishes juvenile

The inconsistency of rewards and punishments has taught the juvenile that there is no relation between breaking or obeying rules and punishment or rewards. Since there are no consequences for good or bad behavior, then it simply doesn't matter what the juvenile does, because punishment is random. If the juvenile justice courts deal out random punishment, then the youth will learn a bitter lesson that behavior is not related to consequences. If juveniles are to learn responsible, moral behavior, punishments have to be fair, consistent and proportional to the rule-breaking behavior.

There are many parenting programs that are helpful. Once again, **Tough love** is one program for parents that have helped with especially troubled and rebellious children. The basic approach is to show that the adults are in charge of their children. No matter how tough the child, the adults have to be in charge of their own home. The adults have to teach their children that everyone is responsible for the consequences of their own behavior. Tough love supplies meetings and support groups for parents with these difficult and sometimes violent children.

Another approach **is Parent Effectiveness Training** with the emphasis on active listening. Parents and guardians need to take time, every day, to listen to their children. **P.E.T.** emphasizes a positive approach much like Carl Roger did. Parents listen carefully to the child. The parent then tells the child what the parent heard. The child corrects any missed meaning and they go back and forth until there is agreement. This non-threatening approach often opens up new communication channels between parents and children. (Gordon, 1970)

The first rule of active listening is to listen positively to your child. For example, the child says, "I don't like my teacher." The parent would say, "You don't like your teacher?" If that doesn't work, then the parent can ask the child why the child doesn't like the teacher. The parent then listens patiently without offering any suggestions until the child is done. Once the child gives the reasons why he doesn't like his teacher, the parent says the reasons back and asks the child if the parent had it right. No judgment is made by anyone at this time because the object is to open up communication and not shut it down. Try it yourself, with your child or a friend. You might be surprised at the change in meanings. It really does work.

Whole Family Therapy

A constant theme of our approach is treating the whole family rather than the individual. In our family chapter we emphasized this. Family therapy is also a counseling approach and we are including it here to emphasize this approach.

The whole family needs to be treated rather than individuals. The case method of social work, counseling, psychology and psychotherapy generally treats individuals as cases, rather than family dynamics as a whole. After every intervention, including taking the youths out of the home, most youths come home to the family and their old neighborhood. A multiple problem family often has a negative influence on juveniles. If there is no intervention and counseling for the family, the youth will continue to get into trouble.

Accepting family therapy is a tough decision for parents and guardians. There is a cost to the parents in time, effort, possibly some loss of family privacy. Many parents may feel that their authority in their own home is being threatened. Some parents feel that this cost is too high and will not allow professionals to intervene. When this happens, there is a high cost to the troubled youth. Some solutions may be fairly simple like learning how to do a family budget, setting aside time for homework or teaching the adults active listening skills so they can understand their children's point of view. Good therapists and counselors provide families with many positive suggestions that are often extremely helpful. It really helps to get an objective opinion from experienced professionals.

Placing Juveniles in Institutions v. Community-Based Programs

Placing juveniles in institutions has proved to be very costly and at times, abusive. The research for avoiding placements in juvenile institutions has been overwhelming for over fifty years. The chance of youths getting into further trouble after being placed in institutions compared to community-based programs has been about the same, no matter how the programs are measured. A bibliography is provided if you want to look at some of the research but it will not change the results. (Lundam, 1993, 2001, Sherman's Web Site) www.ncjrs.gov/works

Group homes have a wide range of environments. Some group homes become too inflexible and controlling with their rules. Some group homes lack enforced rules. Group homes need to provide loving care, counseling and consistently enforced, reasonable and fair rules. There should be a limit of no more than ten juvenile residents. There is a need for 24-hour care, with direct lines to law enforcement. Interventions beyond group counseling should be provided including individual counseling, vocational counseling, job training programs, and education tutors. Group homes are expensive because of the need for 24-hour care, counseling and schooling. Most of the group home youths should be enrolled in an alternate school programs with very small classes of about 10–12 students in each class.

Diversion Although this has been discussed before, diversion as a successful approach deserves a place in this chapter. Diversion tries to use the least restrictive placement for juveniles and to take the juveniles out of the justice system as soon as possible. Diversion programs recommend placement in the juvenile's home along with probation and counseling instead of being placed in an institution or a group home. When evaluating a placement, parents and professionals should always ask the diversion question: "Is this the best and least restrictive placement for this child?"

Area Projects, Street Workers, Social Workers, Community Youth Programs

These approaches have been around for about a hundred years and *include social workers working with juvenile gangs.* A wide variety of neighborhood programs provide recreation, sports programs and counseling for youths. Most of the programs are placed in urban areas where there is high crime and delinquency. Youth workers and social workers are employed by the government to work with youths. Most often, a small number of professionals work with a large number of area youth. The most famous program of this type is the Chicago Area Project. The Chicago Area Project started in the 1930's, with no published evaluations ever and continues to this day, including a summer camp. There have been nationwide evaluations and smaller data-based evaluations, which have shown little or no significant impact on delinquency. There are many fine neighborhood programs that provide good legitimate outlets for youths and are solid alternatives to hanging around doing drugs, alcohol and trouble. Even if neighborhood programs do not reduce delinquency, they are generally a positive influence on the community and should be supported.

Three Programs That *Do Not* Work

D.A.R.E.—*Drug Abuse Resistance Education*

D.A.R.E. and all drug prevention education based on **teaching fear**—*do not work.* Daryl Gates, Chief of the Los Angeles Police Department from 1979–1992 created D.A.R.E. in the early 1980's. He had a son who was addicted to drugs. D.A.R.E. seeks to prevent marijuana, alcohol and cigarette use by elementary school children in 5th and 6th grades. Many hundreds of thousands of dollars has been spent on D.A.R.E. while hundreds of police officers have taught D.A.R.E. programs, which involve thousand of students. DARE does not reduce students' use of marijuana, alcohol and cigarettes. Here is the curriculum, which has become a public relations "feel good" program for police departments (Lundman, 2001:71,91, Sherman, 1998:8)

The 17-Week D.A.R.E. Course

1. Introducing D.A.R.E.
2. Understanding the effect of mind-altering drugs
3. Considering consequences
4. Changing beliefs about drug use
5. Learning resistance techniques—ways to say no
6. Building self-esteem
7. Learning assertiveness—a response style
8. Managing stress without using drugs
9. Reducing violence
10. Combating media influence on drug use and violence
11. Making decisions about risky behavior
12. Saying yes to positive alternatives
13. Having positive role models
14. Resisting gang and group violence
15. Summarizing D.A.R.E. lessons
16. Taking a stand on the use of drugs
17. D.A.R.E. culmination

Scared Straight

This program started by taking middle class suburban adolescents to Rahway State Prison in New Jersey to be interviewed by convicted murderers, armed robbers, rapists and other felons who used obscenity, degradation and threatening behavior to scare the adolescents (1976 to the present). The purpose was to lower delin-quency even though these juveniles were not delinquents. This pro-gram has been used throughout the country with thousand of delinquents and ordinary adolescents. One program had the dra-matic title, J.O.L.T., Juvenile Offenders Learn Truth. In one case, at least, the program encouraged delinquency since the tough students used the inmates as role models. Students should never be exposed to such a degrading experience.

The American Correctional Association has endorsed Juvenile Boot Camps

They include much the same physical endurance as an army boot camp with tough military discipline, yelling, and insulting sergeant types, forced marches and many push-ups for punishments. They also include counseling programs with intense programs for alco-hol and drug abuse, literacy and vocational education. Although there were positive results in literacy and vocational training, boot camps *do not reduce delinquency*. Six-month boot camps for adults have the same rate of return to prison as two years of a routine adult incarceration according to a number of evaluations. Youth simply should not be subject to this degrading program.

The Government Accounting office in a 2007 report on boot camps was concerned with death and abuse. These include dehy-dration, internal bleeding and high blood temperature that related to the death of juveniles. (apnews.myway.com/article/20071013 /d85s883800/html)

Restitution

Proponents say paying restitution teaches responsibility. There is evidence that restitution reduces delinquency. An evaluation of six programs from 1977–1981 showed that restitution reduced delin-quency measured by fewer arrests of juveniles than a comparison group with no restitution. A 1996 report on the evaluation of four restitution programs showed that restitution and probation lowered delinquency more than probation alone. Restitution can be community service, cash to repay damages done to a victim or direct service to a victim. Restitution was originally proposed as an alternate to probation or incarceration but instead was added on to regular probation sentences in all 50 states. About 95% of juveniles successfully completed their restitution according to the research. Utah studied 13,000 restitution cases and found in a 1991 published report a slight (4–7 percent) reduction in delinquency of those who paid restitution compared to those who served routine probation without restitution. Most of the cases were burglary and theft. Having juveniles pay back the victims and community is a major principle of restorative justice. Restorative justice wishes to restore any damage to a community by criminal activity. **The conclusion is that restitution works.**

Regular Probation and Intensive Probation

Regular Probation

Probation is the major Juvenile Justice approach to juvenile counseling for most juveniles. This is why probation appears multiple times. Juvenile probation has normal caseloads of 35–50 youths including mostly office interviews, supplemented by parent, work and school conferences and visitations. Routine probation works reasonably well in keeping most troubled youths from becoming more involved with the juvenile justice system. Once released from probation very few ordinary delinquents continue their involvement in petty crime. Petty crime would be skipping school (truancy), shoplifting, running away from home, occasional drug experimentation and some alcohol abuse. The five percent or so that are repeat offenders often become more involved in crime and drug and alcohol abuse. These are the exceptions to the other 95% of ordinary delinquents.

Intensive Probation

Caseloads are smaller than regular probation, usually twenty-five or less consisting of deeply troubled delinquents. Intensive probation has been used as an alternative to incarceration and evaluations show that both approaches reduce delinquency at about the same rate. However, probation cost is far less than incarceration and keep the juveniles in their own home. According to the research, with smaller caseloads, the probation officers have more time to interact with the youths and supervise the youths. The emphasis is on controlling the juvenile's behavior and protecting the community from the juvenile delinquent.

Rather than lowering delinquency overall, the small caseloads may give the officer more time to violate the youths, especially for technical violations. Technical violations would be not giving the probation officer a change of address or job change on a timely basis. The juveniles could then be sent to group homes or more likely, incarceration. Rather than helping troubled youth, these "violated" youths became more involved in the criminal justice system. These programs started in the 1960's with the California Youth Authority and continue on today all across the country with much the same results. One of the issues is the need for specific training for the smaller caseloads and the utilization of a variety of services. Some examples would be drug and alcohol counseling and anger control programs. Most intensive supervision programs are never evaluated.

Intensive Supervision of Probation (ISP) and Intensive Probation Programs (IPP) may be useful for violent youths and youths deeply involved in crime and drugs as an alternate to incarceration. According to the research, smaller caseloads do not reduce delinquency compared to normal caseloads.

In-School and After-School Programs

Teaching clear, consistent middle class norms and civility, including social skills has lowered delinquent behavior. Examples of social competency skills would be stress management, self-control, anger control, and problem-solving. Actual examples of communication social skills taught to delinquents are: not interrupting all the time and taking turns talking. Larry Sherman reported on his 550-page research web site that an after-school program at a Canadian public housing project really worked. For 32-months low income children age 5 to 15 were involved in after-school sports, dancing, music and scouting. Juvenile arrests declined 75% while arrests in a comparison site rose 67%.

School Violence

One of the most famous acts of high school violence took place at Columbine High School near Denver, Colorado. On April 20, 1999 two male students 16 and 17 killed 12 students, wounded 23 others and then committed suicide. They wore "Gothic" black trench coats and were masked. They carried explosives, one handgun, two shotguns and a rifle into the school. The recommended best answer to this behavior was swift response teams of especially trained police in "disaster response". They should be heavily armed and set up a perimeter. The school should be immediately evacuated. If hostages are taken, an expert hostage negotiation team needs to be on the scene. This takes a great deal of cooperation between the school and the police and a great deal of prior planning.

This is terrifying behavior but it is not the reality in most schools. Violence, school crime and student drug use has been on the decline for over a decade. Students are generally safer at school than away from school. About 90% of schools report no murders and there are less than 100 school related murders nationally. Around 78% of schools have formal school violence programs.

Some urban schools with a history of gang violence in the area have police officers stationed in the schools. These schools also use metal detectors and personal security alarms for teachers. Many schools limit access to the schools and have all visitors sign in to a permanent document. All teachers should attend training with police officers on disaster training, anger prevention and therapeutic restraint. All schools should be equipped with two-way speakers in every room of the school. Student picture identification documents are beginning to appear at schools around the country. Intervention programs with social isolates may be useful and bullying suppression programs may prove of some use. Examining adolescent web sites will often give investigators an idea of what is happening at a school.

Bullying

Bullies tend to become delinquents and become involved in violent behavior. Victims have poor grades and may drop out of school. Schoolwide anti-bullying programs can reduce bullying behavior by 50% within two years as reported by students. Schoolwide programs include enforced rules against bullying especially in the classroom and during school assemblies. Preventing bullying includes individual intervention and counseling with both bullies and victims, class discussions on bullying and meeting with parents.

Mentoring and Community Involvement

The "Community In Schools" program had a positive result in keeping troubled youths in school. It provides caring adult mentors, a safe place to learn and a job skills program in a traditional school. Alternate schools may also use this approach.

Community volunteers mentor and tutor students. Social services may intervene. Students may also get involved in community service. Conflict resolution and violence abatement programs are usually included. While most of these students were at risk for dropping out of school, the program resulted in roughly 80% staying in schools or graduating.

Big Brother and Big Sister programs have a positive effect on juveniles and are well-liked nationally. These programs are about to serve about two hundred thousand children in all fifty states. There are no evaluations that show any reduction in delinquency for these mentor programs. Even though mentor programs have no proven effect on delinquency, they are excellent support programs for students at risk of dropping out of school. There is research that shows that school dropouts are more likely to get more involved in crime and selling drugs.

Curfews have worked in reducing delinquency. Dallas tried a curfew and juvenile victimization dropped by 14%. Chicago's "Time Out" curfew resulted in a 20% crime decrease in a high crime area, while New Orleans aggressively enforced curfew and saw a 27% decrease in youth crime. If your community wants to try out a curfew program, evaluate the results and see if it worked. If curfews do not work for your community, abolish the curfew.

Gangs increase the seriousness and number of criminal and violent activities by juveniles according to the research. In some cities, juvenile gang activity account for 80% or more of serious juvenile crime. Murders by gang members are more likely with or without a drug connection. Two approaches have worked. The first approach is to focus all federal, state and local probation and social workers, district attorneys, and judges on reducing gun violence by juvenile gang members. This includes aggressive prosecutions using state and federal laws. Using this approach, the **Boston Gun Project** reduced gun use by violent juvenile gang members in Boston, Massachusetts by 50% over a three-year period. There have been attempts to replicate the Boston approach in other communities with some success. The second approach is **anger replacement therapy**, which was reported by Larry Sherman to result in a decrease in the arrest of gang members. Anger replacement programs have students keep a diary of their anger behavior and gives specific strategies to curb anger episodes, along with counseling. It is a very positive program.

Camps, Upward Bound and Wilderness Programs These programs may have a positive effect on delinquents in terms of teaching them responsibility and teamwork. The research does not show that these programs reduce delinquency. The best of these programs have long-term follow-ups with the delinquents after they return home. One of the largest programs is Visionquest, which has wilderness camps, sailing and wagon train trips. It has a confrontational style that doesn't let the juvenile get away with anything. The program only takes juveniles who are placed in Visionquest programs by the juvenile courts. These programs have come under severe criticism in terms of victimizing adolescents with harsh confrontational behavior and physical work beyond an adolescent's capacity. The experience and premise is excellent. However, it is necessary to closely examine how the programs actually work and if they treat adolescents with civility and dignity.

How Evaluations Work

The goals for these programs are to help troubled youth and delinquent juveniles by reducing delinquency. Millions of dollars have been spent on these projects over many years. Evaluations are based on scientific principles using empirical data. Most juvenile projects are never scientifically evaluated. In most cases no one knows if most projects work. The Juvenile Justice Guide has searched out programs that show the most promise using the scientific method and empirical evidence.

One approach to evaluations is the *suppression effect*. This shows the suppression of the arrest of juvenile offenders for new crimes. Recidivism looks at juveniles coming back to the juvenile courts, being arrested again or returning to incarceration, after involvement in a program. Best practices are the recommendations of a large number of juvenile justice professionals who have used these programs. Pre- and post-evaluations of program interventions using a comparison group are the standard empirical approach. Large statically significant samples, multiple interviews, longitudinal studies and self-reported offender studies are other approaches that are used. A combination of evaluation techniques is the most effective approach.

Conclusions and Recommendations

Larry Sherman and his team of researchers published in 1998 a 550-page report on the World Wide Web. They made the following recommendations, which still make sense and are based on scientific standards of research (www.ncjrs.gov/works/).

At-risk neighborhoods have the following characteristics:

1. criminal and violent neighbors with
2. drug and alcohol abuse problems,
3. a large percentage of single mothers on welfare and
4. a large number of unemployed males.

By middle class standards, the *Juvenile Justice Guide* means the values of civility, hard work, community service, belief in the law, honesty and respect for people and property with the social skills needed to make these values work in the real world. The following are direct quotes from Sherman's Web Site (www.ncjrs.gov/works/).

Sherman's Recommendations

- helping families to establish clear and consistent discipline and emotional bonding, using home visits and preschool involvement from early infancy

- helping schools to establish a capacity for self-regulation of student conduct with clear norms and expectations, as well as adequate physical security

- helping labor markets to raise labor force participation rates in the neighborhood from 20% to 80%,

- using physical and other place-based prevention to reduce opportunities for crime,

- using massive increases in neighborhood police patrols (and respectful interactions with youth) to get guns off the streets and maintain high standards of civil conduct in public places, and

- using courts and corrections to provide highest priorities to cases arising from these neighborhoods for effective treatment and control of convicted offenders.

Applying Theories

These are based on the three major influences on a juvenile's life: family, neighborhoods and the schools. Delinquent theories support the outcomes of many of these programs.

Control theory requires juveniles to have a stake in the community through jobs, school and family. Ecological theory stresses the influence of improved neighborhoods and ethical role models. Differential Association stresses the need for exposure to legitimate values and norms, including family, friends and associates with legitimate values. Differential opportunity by the theorist Robert Merton shows the need for opportunity and means to learn legitimate skills. This includes a good education and having the goal of gaining access to good job opportunities. These jobs which Merton calls institutional means, provide opportunities where you can make a reasonable living with affordable medical care and a retirement with dignity (Merton's cultural goals).

Routine Activity Theory stresses the need for legitimate guardians to look after juveniles. Psychological theories show how successful juveniles can defer gratification by working hard to save for a better future, and by graduating from school, rather than dropping out. This has also been called the Protestant ethic of Max Weber where you work hard and are rewarded by society for your hard work. Delinquents tend to want immediate gratification so they may drop out of school and steal for the immediate satisfaction of having unearned cash money to spend on themselves. Once you put these theories in normal language in a positive manner, they can make sense for ordinary people as many of these programs show.

Conclusion

Look over the programs and see what may help a certain juvenile, family, neighborhood or school and try it out. If it works, keep it, if it doesn't, try a different program. Not every program will work for each juvenile, family, or neighborhood but a combination of positive programs may really help. A school program may help students who would drop out of school, to stay in school. This may or may not lower delinquency in the community. We can only do the best we can for these future adults. After all, these youths are the future of our country.

10

Updating Juvenile Justice

We have prepared this Guide for parents, juveniles and practioners to show how the juvenile justice system works both legally and in reality. It gives an historical perspective of the American juvenile justice courts system illustrating the difference between the adult criminal justice courts and the juvenile or family courts. Court cases that give juveniles constitutional adult rights are detailed along with cases that deny juveniles certain basic adult rights. Counseling approaches, juvenile program and delinquency theories that make sense and work for some juveniles are also described. The approach to juvenile justice is to encourage positive behavior rather than simply to punish juveniles.

Recommendations

This Guide will help parents and professionals affect juvenile negative behavior to positive behavior. Parents need to take positive steps to become involved with the court process. Many juvenile judges use this positive approach and we applaud them. Furthermore, parents and guardians need to be encouraged by the courts to become part of the juvenile court process of helping place their children in programs, counseling and institutions that meet the juveniles' needs. *Juvenile justice needs to fund programs that actively involve parents and guardians in rehabilitation and the justice process.*

Children and adolescents have to have more, rather than fewer protections from the courts and community and institutional corrections. Due process protection for adults along with the protection of our constitutional bill of rights should be applied to juveniles as well as adults. For example, **all juveniles should have a right of trial by jury of their peers including public trials open to the press and public.** These public trials are needed to insure fair play for both juveniles and adults.

Closing juvenile courts to public scrutiny has been based on an unproven theory called labeling theory. The unproven assumption is that if you label a child or adolescent as a bad person, they will be driven to criminal behavior. This has never been proven! This is the labeling hypothesis based on a forty-year-old myth.

Children and adolescents should have the constitutional right of bail. They would then be placed in the custody of responsible adults. The courts have denied children and adolescents have been denied adult constitutional rights for too many decades. *Children and adolescents should never be executed in any civilized country* and it is about time that the United States Supreme Court agreed.

Court appointed lawyers, law guardians and juvenile judges need at least *five years of full time juvenile court experience.* No one wants "on the job training" while practicing law on children. **Juvenile judges and juvenile court lawyers should go through a certification process.** Juvenile court is a very tough job and most of the judges and juvenile lawyers work very hard to give our children services, justice and fair play. These suggestions will improve the juvenile justice experience for our families and children.

Law should mandate a course of formal training by the states and the juvenile justice bar for all juvenile judges and juvenile court lawyers. As you can see from this Juvenile Justice Guide, juvenile courts are different from adult courts, and judges and lawyers need to learn this. To be fair to our children, judges and lawyers must be familiar with placement choices that are available and what programs work and do not work. In-service training for a minimum of ten hours of professional training every two years is consistent with other lawyer bar standards.

Judges and juvenile court lawyers should be mandated by law to visit a minimum of two juvenile placements a year. For years the juvenile justice system has been sending adolescents to placements that they know very little or nothing about. It is time for a professional-led change in training and standards. We call on the Judicature Society, The American Bar Association. Probation and Parole Officers Association and the juvenile justice and family court bars to endorse these minimum standards. Juvenile court has been neglected for too long. The time is now to upgrade juvenile justice professional and legal standards. In some states and jurisdictions various training and visitation standards have been implemented. Our recommendation is to have universal standards and training for legal guardians, juvenile judges, juvenile court attorneys and foster parents.

Law schools should teach more courses on the juvenile courts and juvenile law. These courses need to focus on juvenile delinquents and persons in need of supervision rather than just family law. Family law often focuses on divorce and separation, which is an important part of the law but does not involve juvenile justice. This would be a positive step to improve law practice in the area of juvenile justice

Children are our most important and vulnerable resource and are the future of our nation. Justice and resources for our children who are in trouble should be a top priority for the United States and its court system. Juvenile courts need the full support of the local community and state and national governments. Criminal justice faculty in colleges and universities has pointed out the need for reform. More resources should be provided for the juvenile justice system.

Meanwhile, juvenile courts in the United States have become somewhat more punishment-oriented over the years. The 1967 U.S. Supreme Court case In Re Gault, by giving juveniles more adult constitutional rights, made the juvenile court more like a criminal court. The first juvenile court was established in 1899, and now, over a hundred years later, we are missing the point of the reason for our juvenile courts. The reason was positive, to help reform and rehabilitate our juveniles so they can become future contributing citizens in the local community. We don't want to just punish juveniles. We want to help them, through their family and community services, become contributing citizens to our community life. Let us return our juvenile justice system to this ideal, fund the system and juvenile defense lawyers professionally and give them the important status they deserve.

Juvenile Justice System Process
A Synopsis

Step One: Apprehension, Arrest and Referral

Person in Need of Supervision (PINS) *(For a status act that is not an adult crime)*	1. Parental Complaint 2. School Complaint 3. Agency Complaint 4. Citizen Complaint
Juvenile Delinquent (JD) *(For a delinquent act that would be an adult crime)*	1. Police Apprehension/Arrest 2. Citizen Complaint

Step Two: Diversion and Probation Intake

Police Agency & Police Youth Bureau	1. Limited Counseling 2. Detention 3. Release 4. May be referred to probation intake or juvenile court 5. Referral for a Detention Hearing in Juvenile Court
Youth Court *(Part of a Diversion program)*	1. Counseling 2. Community Service 3. Restitution to victim 4. May be referred to probation intake or juvenile court

Step Two: Diversion and Probation Intake (continued)

Probation Agency Intake *(Official Government Agency)*	1. Diversion 2. Youth Services including counseling 3. Adjusted successful case and release 4. Terminated Without Adjustment (unsuccessful case and release) 5. Terminated Without Prejudice including Complaint withdrawn 6. Referral to Juvenile Court
Probation Department	1. Intake or Intake/Diversion Unit deals with Diversion and Diversion Release 2. Petition Preparation Unit prepares petitions to send juveniles, including persons in need of supervision and juvenile delinquents, to Juvenile Court before a judge for a Fact Finding Hearing (like an adult criminal trial). 3. Government Attorney may review Juvenile Delinquency, Designated Felony and Transfer Petitions, the last used to send juvenile delinquents to adult criminal court. They are reviewed for legal sufficiency and duplication.

Step Three: Juvenile Court

1. Petition	PINS or JD: Petition is formally filed with Juvenile Court
2. Initial Appearance: Court Intake	a. Determines jurisdiction b. With attorney, respondent admits or denies the facts c. Court Assigned Counsel d. Tests may be ordered on mental capacity e. Probable cause hearing for juvenile delinquents f. May be referred to probation for services and adjustments
3. Fact Finding Hearing	a. Respondent did or did not do the act b. Respondent may admit to the charge, a lesser charge or deny the charge c. Case may be dismissed, or respondent may be adjudicated a JD of PINS d. This is a Judge Trial based on proof beyond reasonable doubt
4. Dispositional Hearing	a. Probation supervision, treatment or confinement b. May be proceeded by a Court Hearing to explore placement. The adjudicated juvenile may be remanded to Social Services or other public or private agencies services and a place to live. c. Juveniles are referred to mental health when there is evidence of a mental disease or defect.

After adjudication, and before the disposition hearing, the probation department will do an investigation concerning placement. The recommendation for placement to the court may come from an individual Probation Officer or a Placement Committee, which may include mental health agencies and social services. Psychometric and psychiatric evaluations called diagnostic assessments can take place by Court Order and must take place for some specific felony adjudications, depending on state law. There may be an evaluation by a Committee on the Handicapped, if there is a disability.

This various hearing in juvenile court may take place in one hearing or over a number of days or weeks. The assigned counsel or law guardian is a lawyer paid for by the government and representing the juvenile, and does not represent the parents or guardians. A juvenile's age for juvenile court jurisdiction is the age that the crime or status offense took place. New York State calls Juvenile Court by the title Family Court.

Step Four: Juvenile Court Dispositions/Sentencing

ACD Adjournment in Contemplation of Dismissal	Up to six months but may be one year
Conditional Discharge	Up to one year
Suspended Judgment	Up to one year
Probation	Up to one year but may be extended to 2 years

Step Four: Juvenile Court Dispositions/Sentencing (continued)

If the juvenile does not fulfill the conditions of the disposition, the juvenile will be ordered to appear in Juvenile Court under a variety of legal procedures with the outcomes determined by the juvenile judge.

ACD Adjournment in Contemplation of Dismissal	Petition for Restoration is brought to Juvenile Court
	Case dismissed at the end of a specific period of time
Conditional Discharge	Revocation based upon a violation is brought to Juvenile Court
	Adjudicated Juvenile is discharged at the end of a specific period of time
Suspended Judgment	Revocation based upon a violation brought to Juvenile Court
	Case dismissed at the end of a specific period of time
Probation	Revocation for a violation of probation is brought to Juvenile Court
	Adjudicated Juvenile is discharged at the end of a specific period of time which may include early discharge and the expiration of probation

Step Five: *Juvenile Court Placements*

Includes State, County and City Departments of Social Services, Probation, Youth and Family Agencies

---

1. Intake and placement planning

2. Direct Counseling Services including after-school programs

3. Direct services to a Juvenile's family

4. Placement in various facilities includes public government agencies, private volunteer agencies and foster care. This includes a wide variety of placements such as secure institutions and residential centers, group homes, nonsecure placements, community placements, wilderness programs, mental health, other state and out-of-state agencies.

5. Juveniles are placed in their own homes on probation with supervision and counseling by probation offices. Counseling may include social workers and programs such as anger control, baby care and parenting skills for young mothers, alcohol abuse and drug counseling programs. Tutoring in academic subjects may also be provided.

6. Aftercare Services provide counseling after the juvenile has been placed in an institution and then returned home.

Glossary

ACD, Adjournment In Contemplation of Dismissal The juvenile judge suspends the case, usually for six months. If the juvenile has not gotten into more trouble, that is, has not come to the attention of the court, the case is dismissed. The juvenile judge may or may not put any conditions on suspending the case. See also conditional discharge and suspended judgment which are used in various states in much the same manner as ACD.

Accepting the Facts is a guilty plea by a juvenile in juvenile court. Not Accepting the Facts is a plea of innocence in juvenile court.

Adjudication This is when the juvenile court judge in a formal action decided whether a juvenile committed an offense or did not commit an offense. See fact-finding.

Adult is a person who is of sufficient age to be responsible for herself or himself, can legally have consensual sex and sign legally enforceable contracts. The age of adulthood differs from state to state for different purposes, and may be before the age of 21. All states agree the age of 21 as adulthood.

Alleged means that someone is accused of a crime. After a conviction for an adult, or an adjudicated for a juvenile, the media and the press need to stop overusing the word alleged, since it has been proven in a court of law that the accused did the crime.

Arrest This is normally when a person or youth is taken into custody by a police officer.

Behavior Modification is based on the stimulus-response and reinforcement psychological model. Tokens and points reward the residents with increasing freedom of movement in the institution, extra visits home and extra desserts. It works well within an institution but does not predict future behavior.

Capital Punishment is when the government of a country kills a juvenile or an adult for committing specific crimes such as murdering somebody. This is also called the death penalty because the juvenile is dead after a capital punishment execution.

Child Abuse is when an adult intentionally harms a child or juvenile, as determined by a criminal court. Examples of physical abuse are burning a child, beatings, sexual assault, tying a child to a bed for days, and can include arm-twisting if there is harm. Psychological and emotional abuse are harder to prove in court, but can be just as damaging with long-term effects as physical abuse.

Child Neglect Parents, guardians and government and private agencies who have care of children have to provide adequate food, clothing, shelter, a stable environment and access to education. If they do not do this, a court can rule that they are neglecting a child or juvenile.

CHINS Children In Need of Supervision, see PINS.

Community Corrections This is an alternative to incarceration or secure detention. A juvenile serves a court disposition (sentence) in a placement usually in their home community or a nearby community. Programs and counseling are normally provided for the youth with the exception of most foster care. Other examples are group homes, enriched foster care, home placement, electronic homebound detention and probation.

Conditional Discharge The release by executive order from a correctional facility of an offender who has not served a full sentence. Examples of conditions to be met are curfew, during the discharge time and staying away from alcoholic beverages. For a variation on this see ACD.

Counselor has two meanings. One meaning is being a state-licensed lawyer. The other is a person who gives psychological analysis and advice. There is generally no licensing requirements in the various states for this type of counselor.

Counseling It is the art of mutually developing, between a counselor and a juvenile, goals that will direct positive future behavior and be carried out. See also therapy and group counseling.

Defense Counsel See juvenile defense lawyer.

Defense Lawyer See juvenile defense lawyer.

Detention Legally authorized confinement of a juvenile by a court while a juvenile is awaiting a juvenile court hearing. By law, this confinement is supposed to be very limited but abuses have crept into the system in a number of jurisdictions. Juveniles have no right of habeas corpus or bail, which allows these problems to persist.

Deterrence is the general theory that fear of punishment will stop people from committing crime. Studies and interviews with criminals show that punishment and fear of punishment including the death penalty, rarely stops anyone from committing crime.

Determinate Sentence is a sentence for a specific period of time, like a two-year sentence.

Disposition is a period of time that the juvenile is under the jurisdiction of the juvenile court. The judge may then place the juvenile under probation or other placement. In adult court this would be called sentencing. See placement.

Diversion is to use alternate approaches to the formal juvenile justice system in order to stop the juvenile from becoming more involved in the system. The first rule, of course, is to do no harm. It would be harming these juveniles and be a waste of services to bring these youths further into the system more than is needed to deal with their problems.

Electronic Homebound Detention is where juveniles are placed in their own home as part of a court ordered disposition (sentence) for a specific period of time with the stipulation that the juveniles can only leave the home for specific reasons. Some examples are school, work, medical and dental services, going to counseling session or seeing a probation officer. The juveniles wear an electronic bracelet or anklet that automatically notifies probation when the juveniles is more than a specific number of feet from the home or if the juvenile tries to remove the bracelet or anklet. This is used more for adults than juveniles.

Ex Parte is a conference in the juvenile judge's chambers between the defense counsel or law guardian representing the child and the prosecuting attorney/lawyer.

Fact Finding This is a hearing in juvenile court before a juvenile judge to determine the facts of a juvenile case. In an adult criminal court this would be a trial to determine guilt or innocence.

Family A traditional family is made up of a mother, father and their children. A family may include other blood relatives such as grandparents and relatives by marriage including cousins and aunts and uncles. It may include non-relatives living in a family household. Many juveniles in poor neighborhoods live with a single mother.

Family Court is the name for juvenile court in New York State. See juvenile court.

Felony This is a serious crime that carries probation or a state prison sentence longer than a year and a day for adults. Examples are armed robbery, drug dealing and murder.

FINS Families In Need of Supervision. See PINS.

Gender is the social characteristics of a male or female identity. Sex is the biological characteristics of a male or female.

Group Counseling also called guided group interaction. A small

Habeas Corpus is Latin "to have the body" and is a fundamental right guaranteed to adults by the U.S. constitution. The court has to produce any adult citizen who is in custody and give a reason for the detention. The U.S. Supreme Court in Schall versus Martin denied this constitutional right to juveniles in 1984. Juvenile courts use preventive detention for juveniles and can lock them up without bail.

I Levels These were called immaturity levels, thus the letter I. However, they really are maturity levels applied originally to juveniles in community corrections in California. These levels have been applied to institutionalized juveniles for many years and used as a basis for extensive counseling and therapy.

Incorrigible generally means that the parents or guardians have lost control over their children because the children will no longer obey the parents or guardians.

Intake This is the unit of a probation agency that initially deals with juveniles. The juvenile may be treated by an intake/diversion unit of probation in an informal manner in a short period of time, or sent on to the juvenile court system for a court hearing. This unit may also refer the juvenile to other private or public counseling agencies, such as social services, testing and counseling for drugs and alcohol dependence and a wide variety of other services.

Indeterminate Sentence is when no specific length, like one year, is given as a sentence. Juveniles cannot be held beyond their 21st birthday if sentenced as a juvenile.

Institutional Services Institutions that deal with juveniles offer counseling, medical and other services to treat juveniles. See secure and nonsecure institution.

JINS Juvenile In Need of Supervision. See PINS.

Jurisdiction means that the Juvenile Justice Court System and Juvenile Judges have the legal ability to make judgments concerning juveniles who have violated the law or committed a non-criminal act defined by law such as not going to school. Jurisdiction is also determined by the age of the juvenile and where the crime or act was committed.

Juvenile is defined age in each state ranging from a low of under sixteen years of age to a high of under twenty-one. Juveniles are not fully legally responsible for their actions.

Juvenile Court has jurisdiction over juveniles who have committed an act that would be a crime if the juvenile were an adult or a status offense. See juvenile delinquent, PINS and status offense.

Juvenile Defense Lawyer This is a state licensed lawyer who represents and defends clients and juveniles in court. Some state appointed lawyers for juveniles are called law guardians.

Juvenile Delinquent A person who has committed an act that would be a crime if that person were an adult. The state laws differ for juvenile court rather than adult court jurisdiction: under age 16 in four states, under age 17 in ten states and under age 18 in the rest of the states. Over the stated ages in the various states

Juvenile Justice is that part of the criminal justice system that deals with juveniles depending on their age and what they did. Unlike the adult system, juvenile justice also deals with acts like running away from home that are not adult crimes. These acts are called status offenses.

Law Guardian This is a state appointed lawyer who represents and defends juveniles and does not represent parents or guardians. See also defense lawyer.

Mediation is a process where juvenile offenders and their victims are brought together by a third party called a mediator to repair and deal with any harm done to the victim. When successful, a mutually agreeable agreement is made between all parties to settle the affair.

Mental Capacity One of the major issues is the ability of the juvenile to really know and understand what is going on in the court session. Some juveniles are too young or immature to understand the court proceedings. Juveniles may have so many emotional and mental problems, or immaturity, that they really do not understand right from wrong.

Mental Health This is where the court is concerned with the emotional and mental abilities of juveniles. Psychological, psychiatric and what are called psychometric tests are often used to find out the mental health of juveniles so that services can be provided.

Milieu Therapy Milieu therapy involves every member of the staff in a residence in therapy including such people as the cooks and janitors. Opening up your innermost feelings with total honesty, communication and listening skills are emphasized to immerse the client totally in the community 24 hours a day, 7 days a week.

MINS Minors In Need of Supervision. See PIN

Misdemeanor is what the court considers as minor offenses in which punishment is limited to short periods of time of less than a year. This punishment could result in local incarceration (institutionalization) or community corrections.

Need Assessment Tries to answer two related questions (1) what does the juvenile need to succeed in life and (2) what does the juvenile need to become a normal and legitimate member of the community.

Neurosis This is a moderate mental illness where the person can still function in society. One example would be fear of heights.

Nonsecure institution This is a placement by a judge in a building that a juvenile can leave at any time. For example, foster care or most group homes.

Parens Patrae This is Latin for the country taking the place of the parents. The theory also applies to judges acting as parents and taking care of the needs of juveniles. This is no longer a popular approach to juvenile justice in the 21st century even though it prevailed in much of the 20th century.

Peers are a group of people who are alike in some way, such as a group of juveniles the same age or social status such as middle class juveniles. Peer group has been used by many to describe a group of equals.

PET (Parent Effectiveness Training) Using active listening skills, parents listen carefully to the child every day. The parent then tells the child what the parent heard. The child corrects any missed meaning and they go back and forth until there is agreement. This non-threatening approach often opens up new communication channels between parents and children.

Petition is a formal written request to a juvenile court for a court hearing for a judgment on a PINS or delinquency alleged behavior by the juvenile. This may include behavior that would be on a misdemeanor or felony level of crime for an adult.

PINS Persons In Need of Supervision is a juvenile who has committed a status offense that is not an adult crime and has been adjudicated by a juvenile court. Various states use various labels such as **CHINS,** Children In Need of Supervision, **FINS,** Families In Need of Supervision, **JINS,** Juvenile In Need of Supervision, **MINS,** Minors In Need of Supervision and **YINS,** Youths In Need of Supervision.

Placement This is when a juvenile court judge decides where to send a juvenile after a placement hearing (sentencing in adult court). Some examples of out-of-home placements are foster care, group homes, secure institutions, etc.

Predisposition Report Before the disposition (sentencing in adult court), the judge needs to have information on the juvenile in order to do what "is best for the child." The probation department prepares this report for the judge, which includes a detailed social history and a recommendation for disposition. See also disposition and social history.

Pre-sentencing Report This is a predisposition report in adult criminal court. See Predisposition Report.

Prevention Detention The court holds the juvenile in custody in a secure or nonsecure institution without bail. This would be unconstitutional for an adult.

Probation is a government agency on the city or county level that is an alternative to incarceration (institutionalization). Probation is part of the community corrections system. This government agency provides a wide range of services to juveniles including counseling and referrals to other public and private social agencies

Psychodrama This is a counseling approach where clients play the roles of significant people in their lives: mother, father, spouse, best friends, enemies, etc. The audience is part of the play and the therapist can be a player.

Psychologists and psychiatrists Psychiatrists also use the term psychotherapy, which may refer to a Freudian approach. Therapy is a fancy word for counseling. Psychologists have a Ph.D. in psychology. Psychiatrists have a medical degree and further professional schooling in the study of the mind and drugs used for such problems as depression. See also counseling.

Psychosis This is a serious mental illness where the person can no longer function normally in society without serious therapy. An example would be manic-depressive, suicidal people.

Rape and Statutory Rape is the forcible penetration of a vagina by a penis, no matter how slight, without consent. Statutory rape may not include physical penetration but is defined by law considering the difference in ages between a child and an adult

Reality Therapy This counseling approach stresses that each youth is responsible for his or her own behavior. The therapist does not accept excuses for bad behavior. Therapy begins with a realistic appraisal of the client's present reality and then plans for the future. The therapist makes moral judgments, and rejects immoral behavior.

Restitution This is where the juvenile pays for any damage done to individuals, or the community, because of the juvenile's bad behavior. Restitution includes money damages, working for a specific person or business and community service. This is a key element in restorative justice.

Glossary

Restorative Justice is an approach to the justice system, which tries to restore a community to where it was before criminal behavior took place. It normally embraces less punitive and more community based initiatives.

Risk Assessment provides a measure of how dangerous to the community and how violent juveniles are. This includes suicidal behavior where the adolescent is a danger to herself or himself as well as trying to predict dangerousness. Basically, professionals rely upon past behavior and some psychometric standardized tests. These predictions of future violent behavior have a history of failure over many years.

Rogerian Non-judgmental Therapy Reframing questions may help develop insight and a positive self-concept according to this approach to counseling, named after Carl Rogers. Rogerian therapy is often used to open up a juvenile in a non-threatening and positive manner. Juveniles genuinely feel better about themselves after experiencing a session with a Carl Roger's trained counselor.

Serious Crimes See misdemeanor and felony. Examples of serious crimes used by legislatures to give adult courts jurisdiction over juveniles are murder, armed robbery, and being a major supplier of illegal drugs such as heroin and crack.

Secure Institution Juveniles are placed in a building involuntarily where the juvenile cannot leave without permission of those in charge of the institution or a court order. There are locks on the doors and windows.

Sentencing See disposition.

Social History This is prepared by probation for a juvenile judge and includes, for example, description of the offense, history of the juvenile's behavior, the juvenile's family, personal traits and strengths, peers and friendships, school, drugs and alcohol abuse, and medical history including emotional and physical disability. See predisposition report.

Social Investigation Report See predisposition report.

Social Worker A government employee providing services to the poor, including counseling, money and referrals to a wide range of agencies. The basic professional degree is a MSW, Master Degree in Social Work on the graduate level.

Special Needs This is a broad category that is used in placement to provide services such as mental health, alcohol and drug counseling, sex therapy and counseling for arsonists. It can refer to physical disabilities such as blindness, heart conditions, health-based special diets and diabetes.

Status Offenses This is a juvenile offense that would not be a crime if the juvenile was an adult and includes skipping school, running away from home, curfew violations, drinking alcoholic beverages outside of the home and most consensual sex acts.

Suspended Judgment See **ACD**

Tough Love This is one program for parents that have helped with especially troubled and rebellious children. The basic approach is to show that the adults are in charge of their children. No matter how tough the child, the adults have to be in charge of their own home. The adults have to teach their children that everyone is responsible for the consequences of their own behavior. Tough love supplies meetings and support groups for parents with these difficult and sometimes violent children.

Transfers have two different definitions. One is transfer to different placements; a juvenile may be transferred from foster care to a secure institution or transferred to an out-of-state institution or back to the juvenile's home. Secondly there is transfer for juvenile court to adult court. See waiver.

Violation Hearing Conditions are set and enforced by the court and probation for dispositions (sentences). When the youth is documented as *not* carrying out these conditions such as a curfew, attending school or a counseling program, then a violation hearing is called for. The youth has a hearing before the juvenile judge in court including having a lawyer representing the juvenile. Facts are presented and the judge makes a decision. The juvenile may be restored to probation, for example, or sent to a juvenile institution.

Waiver is transferring a juvenile to adult court under specific state laws. The juvenile court gives up or waives its jurisdiction over the juvenile. It depends on the juvenile age when the crime took place and the seriousness of the crime, such as murder or armed robbery.

YINS Youths In Need of Supervision. See PINS.

Annotated Bibliography

Acker, James R. and Elizabeth B. Acker. *Two Voices On The Legal Rights of American Youth*. Belmont, Ca.: Wadsworth/Thomson Learning, 2004. This is a comprehensive description of the legal cases on Youths' Rights.

Berne, Eric. *Games People Play*. New York, N.Y.: Grove Press, 1964, republished in 1971. This is the book that started it all: "I'm O.K. You're O.K.".

Braswell, Michael, Tyler Fletcher and Larry Miller. *Human Relations and Corrections*. Third Edition. Prospect Heights, Ill. 1990. An excellent description of counseling approaches for criminals.

Campbell, Anne. *The Girls in the Gang*. Cambridge, Mass.: Blackwell Publishers, 1991. This is the classical work on this topic. Since 1984, first edition, girl gangs have become more violent and deeper into drug distribution.

Champion, Dean J. *Probation, Parole and Community Corrections*. Upper Saddle River, N.J.: Prentice Hall, 2008. This is a popular basic textbook in this field.

Chesney-Lind, Meda and Randall G. Shelden. *Girls, Delinquency and Juvenile Justice*. Pacific Grove California: Brooks/Cole Publishing, 1992. This is the best book in a field that has been sadly neglected by most criminologists.

Crews, Gordon A. and Reid H. Montgomery. *Chasing Shadows*. Upper Saddle River, N.J.: Prentice Hall, 2001. Descriptions, theories and recommended solutions for juvenile violence in America.

Cromwell, Paul. *In Their Own Words*. Los Angeles, CA: Roxbury Publishing, 1999. Criminals in their own words describe their crimes and motivations for committing crimes.

Cromwell. Paul F., Leanne Fiftal Alarid and Richard V. del Carmen. *Community-Based Corrections*. Belmont, CA: Wadsworth/Cengage, 2008. This is a standard textbook in the field with a chapter on juvenile justice.

Annotated Bibliography

Egley, Arlem. Cheryl L. Maxson, Miller and Malcolm W. Klein. *The Modern Gang Leader.* Los Angeles, CA: Roxbury Publishing, 2007. This has a wide selection of gang research and scholarly writing on gangs.

Elliott, Michele. *Female Abuse of Children.* New York, N.Y.: Guilford Pre, 1993. When we had more independent presses, a scholarly book on this subject.

Fields, Jason. *American Families Living Arrangements* U.S. Census Bureau, Current Population Survey, March and Annual Social and Economic Supplements: 1970 to 2003. Issued November 2004, page 1. www.census.gov/prod/2004/p 20-553

Garbarino, James. *Lost Boys.* New York, N.Y.: The Free Press, 1999. This volume on the chilling violence of young men and boys lists the causes and recommendations for remedies. One of the questions he asks is, "How does a soul survive in a world of torment?"

Garbarino, James and Claire Bernard. *Parents Under Siege.* New York, N.Y., 2001. Gives parents tools for parenting, including using empathy and how to deal with "When Bad things Happen to Good Families."

Glasser, William, *Reality Therapy.* New York, N.Y.: Harper and Row, 1975. This is a reissue of the most effective counseling approach to help delinquents deal with their problems and be realistic about their lives and chances in life. Google reality therapy. http://www.wglasser.com/

Goldstein, Arnold P. *Delinquents On Delinquency.* Champaign, Ill.: Research Press, 1990. This book consists of suggestions from delinquents, in their own words on solutions for delinquency. This project took 19 years and went to seven states.

Goldstein, Arnold. *Delinquent Gangs: A Psychological Perspective.* Champaign, Ill.: Research Press, 1991. His work on adolescent behavior and gangs as group behavior is fascinating.

Gordon, Thomas. *Parent Effectiveness Training.* New York: Peter H. Wyde, publisher, 1970. A widely-used effective approach to bringing up responsible children and developing listening skills. Gordon also published Leader Effectiveness Training in 2001, has a website you can google and his books are available at Amazon.com.

Gray, Ellen. *Child Abuse: Prelude to Delinquency.* Washington, D.C.: U.S. Department of Justice, 1984. An early recognition of the link between child abuse and delinquency. For an update, see Larry Siegel's *Juvenile Delinquency* text. Although all abused children do not become delinquent, a large percent of delinquents have been abused as children, an overwhelming statistic. See also the Campbell CCJG web site.

Griffin, Patricia and Patricia Torbet, Eds. *Desktop Guide to Good Juvenile Probation Practice.* Pittsburgh, Pa.: National Center for Juvenile Justice, 2002. This is simply the best practical handbook identifying and describing best practices in the field of juvenile probation.

Heide, Kathleen M. *Young Killers.* Thousand Oaks, CA.: Sage Publications, 1999. The last two chapters give many recommendations on approaches to reducing juvenile violent crime and how to help these violent juveniles. Most of the book is a portrait of young killers, giving a human face to these violent youth.

Inciardi, James A., Ruth Horowitz and Anne E. Pottieger. *Street Kids, Street Drugs and Street Crime.* Belmont, CA.: Wadsworth Publishing, 1993. A powerful and detailed examination of juvenile drug use and juvenile drug dealers in Miami, street level research.

Kennedy, David. "Pulling Levers, Getting Deterrence Right." *National Institute of Justice Journal,* July, 1998. Pp. 5–8. Documents the methods and outcomes of the Boston Gun Project. The same methods were tried in Minneapolis, Minn., D. Kennedy and A. Braga. "Homicide in Minneapolis." *Minneapolis Homicide Studies,* 1998. 2:263-290. See also, D. Kennedy, A. Piel and A. Braga. "Youth Violence in Boston: Gun Markets, Serious Youth Offenders and Use-Reduction Strategies." *Law and Contemporary Problems,* 1996. 59:147-196

Knox, George. *An Introduction to Gangs.* Bristol, Wydham Hall Press, 1994. This 817-page book in small print is the most comprehensive book on gangs in America, today.

Lawrence, Richard. *School Crime and Juvenile Justice.* New York, N.Y.: Oxford, 1998. Specialized field and a useful, needed text, easily out-of-date.

Lee, Duane, George E. Rush an Anthony M. Smith. *Gangs, Graffiti and Violence.* 2nd ed. Incline Village, Nevada: Copperhouse Publishing, 2000. This is a good general description of the various ethnic gangs in America.

Lester, David and Michael Braswell. *Correctional Counseling.* Cincinnati, Ohio, Anderson, 1987. An excellent description of counseling approaches for criminals.

Logan, Sadye, L.M, Ed. *The Black Family: Strengths, Self-Help and Positive Change.* 2nd edition. Boulder, Colorado: Westview, 2001. A terrific series of articles showing the stability and endurance of the Black/African-American family through networking with extended kin, neighbors and friends while living in difficult circumstances. Professor Chuck Willie, of Harvard, first documented this: from Edward A. Thibault's graduate days. You can now find reference to this networking in most introductory sociology textbooks.

Lundman, Richard J. *Prevention and Control of Juvenile Delinquency.* Third edition. New York, N.Y.: Oxford University Press, 2001. A description of the classic programs and placements for juveniles over many decades along with evaluations of the success and failure of these programs.

Lyons, John A. and Edward J. Taylor. *Manual for Probation Officers in New York State.* Fifth edition. Albany, N.Y.: New York State Department of Correction, Division of Probation, 1945. An historical document and comprehensive manual for probation officers including many details and examples that are used today. New York State, generally, does not archive these types of justice documents.

McCorkle, Richard C. and Terrance D. Miethe. *Panic: The Social Construction of the Street Gang Problem.* Upper Saddle River, N.J.: Prentice Hall, 2002. Since most gang members are ages 10-25 and 90% male, gang membership makes up two and a half percent of this male cohort. Gang members talk more violence than they actually do. The media, the police and prosecutors make up the rest of the hype on violent gangs. Fine empirical study set in Nevada.

Mannheim, Herman, ed. *Pioneers in Criminology.* 2nd edition. Montclair, New Jersey, Patterson Smith, 1973. This is the best book of original essays by world-renowned scholars on the major historical theorists in criminology. It is an intellectual history of the field.

Messner, Steven F. and Richard Rosenfeld. *Crime and the American Dream.* Belmont, CA: Wadsworth, 2001. An intriguing theory that the cultural basis for crime in America is getting rich by any means no matter how unethical.

Office of Juvenile Justice and Delinquency Prevention. *Promising Strategies to Reduce Gun Violence.* Washington, D.C.: Office of Juvenile Justice and Delinquency Prevention, 1999. Documents the success of the Boston Gun Project.

Onondaga Probation. *Family Crises Intervention Unit.* Syracuse, N.Y., Onondaga Probation, 1978. An historical first; predating Morton Bard's New York City family crisis intervention program.

Parry, David L. *Essential Readings in Juvenile Justice.* Upper Saddle River, N.J.: Pearson, Prentice Hall, 2005. Major court cases and essential readings in Juvenile Justice.

Piquero, Alex and Paul Maserolle, Eds. *Life-Course Criminology.* Belmont, Ca.: Wadsworth/Thompson, 2001. The difference between adolescent delinquency and career criminality is emphasized. Almost all adolescents becoming more mature and stop their criminal behavior as they approach age thirty. Career/chronic adult criminals continue living in a poor neighborhood after being marginalized in school during adolescence. Early aggressiveness seems to be stable from childhood to adulthood.

Rice, E. Philip. *Intimate Relationships, Marriages and Families.* Third Edition. Toronto, Canada: Mayfield Publishing, 1996. A college textbook that includes alternate family styles.

Ricci, Isolina. *Mom's House, Dad's House; Making Shared Custody Work.* New York, N.Y.: Collier/Macmillan, 1980. Still the best book for divorced parents and their children.

Schmallenger, Frank and Clements Bartollas *Juvenile Delinquency.* Upper Saddle River, N.J.: Prentice Hall, 2007. A fine textbook by two of the best authors in criminal justice. Schmallenger has a reputation for being up-to-date with great web sites.

Shoemaker, Donald. *Theories of Delinquency.* Fourth edition. New York, N.Y.: Oxford University Press, 2000. This is a clear explanation of the standard theories of delinquency in paperback.

Annotated Bibliography

Short, James F., Lorrie A. Hughes and Henry Pontell. *Juvenile Delinquency and Delinquents: The Nexus of Social Change*. Upper Saddle River, N.J.: Prentice Hall, 2008.

Siegel, Larry, Brandon C. Welsh and Joseph Senna, *Juvenile Delinquency: Theory, Practice and Law*. Ninth Edition. Belmont, Ca.: Wadsworth/ Thomson Learning, 2006. The best-documented and comprehensive college text on juvenile justice and juvenile delinquency.

Schmallenger, Frank. *Criminal Justice Today*. Ninth edition. Upper Saddle River, N.J.: Pearson, Prentice Hall, 2007. Best and most up-to-date introduction to criminal justice with great web sites.

Sherman, Larry, et al. *Preventing Crime: What Works, What Doesn't Work, What's Promising*. Washington, D.C.: U.S. Government Office, 1998. Best summation of research in criminal justice at that time. See also the website.

Snyder, Howard N., Melissa Sickmund and Eileen Poe-Yamagata. *Juvenile Transfers to Criminal Court in the 1990's: Lessons Learned from Four Studies*. Washington, D.C.: Officer of Juvenile Justice and Delinquency Prevention, 2000. Provides a nice review of the U.S. v. Kent criteria and empirical data on transfer from juvenile to adult court.

Straus, Murray A. and Richard J. Gelles. *Physical Violence in American Families: Risk Factor and Adaptations to Violence in 8,145 Families*. New Brunswick (USA) and London (UK): Transaction Publishing, 1992. Often suppressed and ignored but still the best empirical study on family violence. It had to be published outside of the United States. Except for corporal punishment, further research by this brilliant team was not funded because of its fairness and objectivity to both men and women.

Thibault, Edward, Lawrence M. Lynch and R. Bruce McBride. *Proactive Police Management*. 7th ed. Upper Saddle River, New Jersey, 2007. Gives a description of specific juvenile justice programs and the police, high school violence, etc.

Tracy, Paul E., Marvin E. Wolfgang and Robert Figlio. *Delinquency Careers in Two Birth Cohorts*. New York, N.Y.: Plenum Press, 1990. The most famous delinquency cohort studies of recidivism in Philadelphia.

Annotated Bibliography

Van Voorhis, Patricia, Michael Braswell and David Lester. *Correctional Counseling and Rehabilitation*. Cincinnati, Ohio: Anderson Publishing, 1997.

Vold, George B., Thomas J. Bernard and Jeffrey B. Snipes. Theoretical Criminology. 4th edition. *Theoretical Criminology*. New York: Oxford University Press, 1998; 5th edition, 2001. This is simply the best book ever written on criminology theory, on the graduate level.

Wicks, Robert J. *Correctional Psychology*. San Francisco: Canfield Press, 1974. Early review of the applied field of counseling.

Wilson, James Q. and Richard J. Herrnstein. *Crime and Human Nature*. New York, N.Y.: Simon and Schuster, 1985. A terrific best seller. It provides a well-researched recommendation on parenting styles and their outcomes.

Wooden, Wayne S. *Renegade Kida, Suburban Outlaws*. Belmont, CA: Wadsworth Publishing, 2001. One of the very few sources on middle class delinquency.

Wright, Kevin and Karen E. Wright. *Family Life, Delinquency and Crime: A Policymaker's Guide*. Washington, D.C.: Office of Juvenile Justice and Delinquency, 1995. This is a brilliant summary of the research.

Websites

American Bar Association www.abanet.org

Campbell Justice http://www.campbellcollaboration.org
This provides review of recent research on crime and delinquency.

Foundation Directory http://fdncenter.org
This is a major source for thousands of private grants worth millions of dollars.

International Association of Chiefs of Police www.theiacp.org

International City/County Management Association http://icma.org

National Crime Prevention Council www.ncpc.org

National Council on Crime and Delinquency
   www.nccd-crc.org/nccd/n_index_main.html
Founded in 1907, NCCD has been a major force for reform and research in juvenile justice. You can simply google NCCD.

Office of National Drug Policy www.whitehousedrugpolicy.gov

Reality Therapy http://www.wglasser.com/

Research, University of Michigan Institute www.isr.umich.edu/home/

Sherman's Web Site www.ncjrs.gov/works

Tough Love http://www.4troubledteens.com/toughlove.html
Is supportive of the tough love approach for parents.

United States Federal Government Websites
Juvenile Justice Related

US Department of Justice www.usdoj.gov
This is the main site for the Department of Justice and this site gives you access to other DOJ major web sites such as:

   Bureau of Justice Assistance www.ojp.usdoj.gov/bja

   Bureau of Justice Statistics www.ojp.usdoj.gov/bjs

Corporation for National and Community Service www.cns.gov

Office of Juvenile Justice and Delinquency Prevention
   www.ojjdp.ncjrs.org

Federal Bureau of Investigation (FBI) www.fbi.gov

National Criminal Justice Reference Service www.ncjrs.org

National Institute of Justice (NIJ) www.ojp.usdoj.gov/nij
NIJ documents have enriched the authors over these many years.

Office of Juvenile Justice/Office for Victims of Crime
   www.ojp.usdoj.gov/ovc/

US Food and Drug Administration www.fda.gov

US Census Bureau, *American Families Living and Arrangements*
   http://www.census.gov/population/www/socdemo/hh-fam.html
This is the current data on the structure of the America family.

A Note on Websites: We have provided mostly government and solid institutional, trustworthy addresses. Websites change frequently and many have undocumented opinions and data.

Index

Index

Index

Index

Index

strain theory, 107–110

street workers, 128

suicide evaluation, counseling, 46

supervision, 122–123

suspended judgment, 84, 148–149, 151

T

techniques of neutralization, 111

theories, 101–119

therapy

See counseling

tough love, 50–51, 125, 162

transactional analysis, 92–93

transfers, 5, 10, 51, 57–59, 71–72, 76, 146, 162–163

U

United States, Kent v., 69–71

upward bound programs, 136

V̇

violation hearing, 44, 84–85, 163

violent offenders, 47–48

Visionquest, 136

vocational training, 48, 127, 130

V.T.L.O., New Jersey v., 78

W

websites, 173, 175

wilderness programs, 136

Y

youth court, 50, 145

The
JUVENILE JUSTICE GUIDE
by
Edward A. Thibault. Ph.D.
John J. Maceri, M.S.W.

A concise & practical handbook for:

Those involved in the juvenile justice system—

Parents

Juveniles

Professionals

Probation Officers

Juvenile Parole Officers

Police Officers

Lawyers

Social Workers

Youth Workers

Criminal Justice College Students & Faculty

The Perfect Supplemental Text for:

Juvenile Delinquency and Juvenile Justice Courses